Chinese Cookery

'Through cooking you make friends; through eating you enjoy the friendship.' Nancy Chih Ma is one of the world's most famous exponents of Chinese cooking and in this book she conveys the art of real Chinese cooking. Simplicity and economy are the hallmarks of the Chinese cuisine. Meals can be cooked in minutes by quick-frying; steaming, a favourite Chinese cooking method, preserves all the natural juices, flavours and nutrients.

Nancy Chih Ma's easy-to-follow recipes will enable the beginner to Chinese cookery to produce an exquisite and authentic meal. The experienced cook will be delighted by the extensive range and variety of Mrs Ma's recipes.

NANCY CHIH MA

Chinese Cookery

Illustrated by Tony Streek

MAGNUM BOOKS
Methuen Paperbacks Ltd

A Magnum Book

CHINESE COOKERY
ISBN 0 417 02900 4

First published in 1978 by Eyre Methuen Ltd
Magnum edition published 1980

Magnum Books are published by Methuen Paperbacks Ltd
11 New Fetter Lane, London EC4P 4EE

Made and printed in Great Britain by
Hazell Watson & Viney Ltd
Aylesbury, Bucks

Contents

Eggs

Vegetables and Salads

Pastries and Rice

Soups

Desserts

Introduction

The Ingredients

China has the oldest civilisation in the world, and the art of Chinese cooking has been practised for over five thousand years. Its art depends on understanding the Chinese methods of cooking, using ingredients available in any supermarket. Of course, there are special ingredients as well, but all you need are meat, vegetables, soy sauce and oil to start cooking the Chinese way!

Pork is the staple meat in China because it has a fine grain and a delicate flavour. It is used in a great variety of dishes: stir-fried pork, deep-fried pork, steamed pork, barbecued pork, roast pork and ham.

Beef is not eaten as much as in the west, as in China cattle are highly valued for agricultural farming. **Veal** is almost never eaten, and **lamb** only in the Northern Provinces.

Chicken and **duck** are favourite foods, as is **fish**. As well as freshwater fish, all kinds of seafood are found in China, which has a three thousand mile coast-line. Fresh, dried and salted seafood is used in much of the cooking.

China's **vegetables** are similar to the seasonal vegetables of western countries. In addition, many **natural foods** are grown, such as bean sprouts, bean curd, water chestnuts, bamboo shoots, all kinds of mushrooms and beans.

Oil: besides the vegetable oils (corn oil, soy bean oil, olive oil, sunflower oil) sesame oil is much loved, and has a distinctive flavour. If you cannot buy it, it can be made as follows: lightly toast some sesame seeds in a dry pan, then grind them in a blender and mix with salad oil. Lard is an alternative to vegetable oil, but it is better not to use it as it makes the food 'heavier'.

Dried ingredients include poultry, fish, fruits and vegetables, and the most popular of these are mushrooms, bamboo shoots, shrimps, fish, cuttlefish, shark's fin, plums and dates. They are preserved by salting, being dried in the sun or wind, or in sugar or syrup, and most dried food must be soaked before cooking to bring out the full flavour and increase in size. Chinese dried or canned food is fairly expensive, but used sparingly gives good results.

The basic **seasonings** are vegetable oil, soy sauce, ginger, garlic, scallion, Chinese wine (or dry sherry), sugar, salt and pepper. Chilli sauce, star aniseed, mustard, peppercorns and ketchup are also important for flavouring food, and there are also a number of special spices from the various provinces.

Grain: wheat is produced in North China, and the people there eat more noodles, Chinese bread, dumplings, pancakes, pastries and sweet and meat buns than those of South China, where the staple food is rice.

Tea is said to have originated in China around the 4th century B.C. No one really knows how tea-drinking first started, although there is one famous legend of how tea was discovered. Many centuries ago a Chinese scholar was boiling water in the forest. By accident, some leaves fell into the water, making it fragrant. Upon drinking the water the scholar found that although it was bitter, it left a delicate and sweet aftertaste. Most historians, of course, would not vouch for such a legend, but they do believe that tea was first drunk for medicinal purposes and only later drunk as a refreshing beverage. It is usual to drink tea with a Chinese meal, but milk and sugar are never used.

A Chinese meat dish uses only half the quantity of meat used in western dishes, so that it is not only economical but well-balanced with low calories and high nutrients – the Chinese rarely have to diet!

The meal is the family gathering hour, and is the symbol of good life; a time for friendship. Through cooking you make friends; through eating you enjoy the friendship.

Methods of Chinese Cooking

Chinese food is eaten with chopsticks, made from bamboo, ivory, silver, gold or plastic. The knife is never used at the table, so food preparation involves a little time. The ingredients should be cut into tiny pieces (not big chunks), paper-thin or thread-long and mixed together in one dish. It is easier to slice meat thinly if it is partially frozen; it is then marinated before cooking. Poultry should be jointed and you will find it easier to dismember chicken by finding the joints of the legs and wings and inserting a knife at these points. Duck should be cut with a cleaver: cut off the legs at the thigh joints and wings at the shoulder joints, then split the duck down the back to divide it in two. Cut each half into six pieces; wash and wipe. Most Chinese like to keep the skin on poultry as they enjoy the flavour.

Stir-frying: use meat, seafood, vegetables, etc. Cut into slices or dice, mince or shred. Always cut up all the ingredients that will be needed, collect them together and measure out the seasonings in little bowls. As soon as the oil in the pan gets hot, rapidly add the ingredients, stir for a few minutes over a strong flame, add the prepared seasonings, stir again and serve. A fascinating cooking method, as timing is important. The thought should be on the next step, the hand should hold the pan and the other hand should stir with a spatula. The eye should always be on the food.

Deep-frying: first marinate the ingredients with Chinese wine or dry sherry, soy sauce or other spices. Heat plenty of oil to 180C/350F and deep-fry until the food is crisp or golden brown. Sometimes the ingredients are just coated with corn-flour, and egg and flour batter or an egg white batter.

The secret of making food more crisp is to deep-fry it until the food is pale golden, then remove it from the oil and allow it to cool; reheat the oil and return the food to it until the deep-frying is completed. This results in the food being cooked equally inside and out.

Steaming: the Chinese bamboo steamer is an excellent utensil. With two layers in your bamboo steamer you can steam two different dishes at the same time. The steam is absorbed by the bamboo cover so that water never drops into the food. Steam fish, shrimps, meat, chicken and dumplings on a plate in the steamer, and serve directly from it. In this way all the natural juices, flavours and nutrients are preserved.

Braising: like preparing a stew. Stir-fry the food then add the seasonings and stock, bring to the boil and simmer for 1 hour or until everything is tender.

Roastings: marinate large cuts of pork, chicken or duck with soy sauce and Chinese wine or dry sherry, and roast in an oven or barbecue oven. A water container should always be put underneath to take the drippings and prevent them from burning, and to make the meat juicy inside and crisp outside.

Smoking: place the chicken or other meat on a rack. Smoke with tea leaves, brown sugar and star aniseed, cinnamon and other spices to flavour the food.

Mixed salad: after cutting up the salad, toss with seasonings.

Soup: Chinese soup is based on stock. Chicken or pork is usually used (or just the bones) and is simmered for hours. Meat or vegetables can then be added to this stock, and it is served as a soup towards the end of the meal after the main dishes.

Beef and Lamb

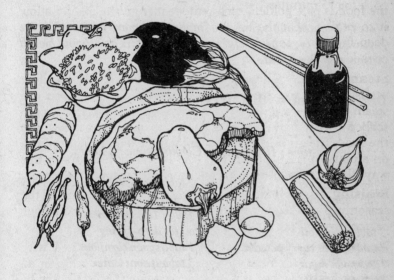

Braised Beef and Aubergine

Preparation time : 40 minutes   *Cooking time : 20 minutes*

225g (8oz) sliced beef	*1 clove of garlic*
1 aubergine	*3 tablespoons oil*
1 tomato	*2 tablespoons soy sauce*
1 green pepper	*½ teaspoon sugar*
1 small onion	*⅓ cup water*

1. Peel the aubergine. Cut lengthwise into quarters then cross-wise into approximately 2½cm (1in) sections. Soak in water to prevent the colour changing to brown. A plate should be

placed on top of the bowl to prevent the sections from floating upwards.
2. Crush the garlic. Cut the tomato into bite-sized pieces. Peel the onion and cut into chunks. Halve the green pepper, take out seeds and cut into bite-sized pieces.
3. Heat a pan and brown the garlic; add the beef and onion. As soon as this changes colour add the vegetables, soy sauce, sugar and water and cover with a lid. Turn the heat low and cook for 15 minutes.

Note : Oriental aubergines are smaller and more tender than the English variety, so be careful not to overcook. They should be soft outside and firm inside.

Braised Beef with Curry

CHA LI CHI

Preparation time : 10 minutes   Cooking time : 2 hours

1¼kg (2¾lb) beef
225g (8oz) onion
4 cloves garlic
5 tablespoons oil
2 tablespoons curry powder
1 teaspoon sugar
2 teaspoons salt

2 tablespoons Chinese wine or dry sherry
450g (1lb) potatoes
oil for deep-frying
1 tablespoon cornflour
3 tablespoons water

1. Cut the beef into 4cm (1½in) chunks; dip into hot water and drain.
2. Crack the garlic. Cut each onion into 8 pieces.
3. Heat the oil, fry the onion and garlic for a few minutes, add the curry powder and stir well. Add the sugar, salt, wine and the beef; cover with sufficient water and simmer over a low flame. Cook the beef for about 2 hours, or until tender.
4. Cut the potatoes into chunks and soak in water for about 5 minutes; drain and dry well. Deep-fry until golden brown.
5. Five minutes before serving, add the potatoes to the beef, and thicken with a mixture of the cornflour and 3 tablespoons of water. The garlic should be removed before serving.

Braised Beef with Tomato

HUNG SHAO FAN CHIEH NIU JOU

Preparation time : 15 minutes   Cooking time : 2 hours

450g (1lb) beef
3 tomatoes
1 clove garlic
1 stalk leek
4 slices ginger

6 tablespoons oil
2 tablespoons soy sauce
1 teaspoon salt
1 tablespoon cornflour
3 tablespoons water

1. Cut the beef into chunks. Heat 4 tablespoons of oil and stir-fry the garlic, leek and ginger. When fragrant add the beef and sauté until its colour changes. Add the soy sauce and salt and sufficient water to cover and cook for 1–2 hours, until the beef is tender.
2. Soak the tomatoes in boiling water for a couple of minutes; remove the skin and cut each tomato into 6 pieces.
3. Heat 2 tablespoons oil and sauté the tomatoes. Mix with the beef and thicken with a cornflour and water mixture. Serve hot.

Deep-fried Beef with Chilli

CHA LA NIU JOU

Preparation and cooking time : 30 minutes

450g (1lb) sirloin steak or lean beef
225g (8oz) celery
110g (4oz) carrot
4 tablespoons oil
oil for deep-frying
1 tablespoon Chinese wine or
   dry sherry
1 tablespoon hot soy bean sauce
1 tablespoon sweet soy bean sauce

3 dried red chilli peppers
2 teaspoons minced garlic
2 tablespoons leek
1½ teaspoons salt
2 teaspoons sesame oil
1 teaspoon sugar
1 teaspoon ginger
½ teaspoon coarsely ground pepper
2 teaspoons hot pepper oil

1. Slice the beef against the grain and shred to matchstick thickness.

2. Remove leaves from celery. Shred in 4cm (1½in) lengths. Peel carrot. Slice and shred to same thickness and length as celery.

3. Crush dried red chilli peppers, remove and discard the seeds. Alternatively soak the dried red peppers in hot water, discard seeds, and shred when they become soft.

4. Chop the leek and ginger finely.

5. Heat 3 tablespoons oil, stir-fry celery and carrot to slightly soften. Add ½ teaspoon salt; remove to a plate.

6. Heat the deep-frying oil and deep-fry the beef for 1 minute; lift out of the oil. Reheat oil and deep-fry for 1 more minute. Repeat process a third time. Drain well.

7. Heat the remaining tablespoon oil; stir-fry the garlic; when fragrant, add the hot soy bean sauce, sweet soy bean sauce, crushed dried red peppers, leek and sesame oil. Mix over hot flame to blend. Return beef and vegetables to the pan. Add ginger, sugar, ground pepper, hot pepper oil and remaining teaspoon salt. Stir well and serve hot.

Note. This is one of the noted Szechuan dishes. The complicated flavour is very unusual. The Chinese say that this dish is good for the health if you live in a wet climate.

Fried Beef with Green Peppers

CHING CHIAO NIU JOU

Preparation and cooking time : 20 minutes

225g (8oz) beef, flank steak	3 green peppers
1½ tablespoons soy sauce	110g (4oz) bamboo shoots
1 teaspoon cornflour	½ teaspoon salt
a dash of black pepper	5 tablespoons oil

1. Slice the beef very thinly against the grain, then sliver into strips.

2. Dredge the slivered beef with the 1½ tablespoons soy sauce, 1 teaspoon cornflour, and a dash of black pepper.

3. Cut off the stem ends of the green peppers and discard. Cut

each pepper in half, remove the seeds, and then cut into thin strips.

4. Slice the bamboo shoots and cut again into slivers.

5. Heat 3 tablespoons oil until very hot. Stir-fry the beef until it just changes colour. Remove to a plate. Do not cook for longer than 2 minutes.

6. Heat the remaining 2 tablespoons oil. Stir-fry the green peppers until they are very hot, about 1 minute; add ½ teaspoon salt and the bamboo shoots.

7. Return the beef to the pan with the vegetables; stir over a high heat for about 1 minute, until all ingredients are very hot. Serve at once.

Note : Other cuts of meat may be used such as round steak, bottom or top round or tenderloin.

Fried Fillet of Beef with Vegetables

CHA LI GI

Preparation time : 15 minutes   *Cooking time : 10 minutes*

450g (1lb) fillet of beef, sliced into 36 pieces	Seasonings
7 tablespoons oil	4 tablespoons soy sauce
450g (1lb) spinach, cut into sections	2 tablespoons Chinese wine or dry sherry
½ teaspoon salt	1 teaspoon ginger juice
	1 teaspoon sugar
	a dash of black pepper

1. Soak the beef slices in the seasonings for 10 minutes.
2. Heat 4 tablespoons oil and stir-fry the beef.
3. Heat 3 tablespoons oil, add salt and stir-fry the spinach until it becomes tender.
4. Place the fried spinach on a plate and spread the fried beef over it. Pour the juice from the fried beef over spinach and beef and serve.

Note : Spinach can be substituted with 225g (8oz) snow peas (remove the ends).

Stir-fried Sliced Beef

CHAO SHIAN PEI

Preparation time : 15 minutes   Cooking time : 5 minutes

450g (1lb) sliced beef
4 tablespoons soy sauce
1 tablespoon sesame oil

1 teaspoon sugar
1 leek or onion, chopped
3 tablespoons cooking oil

1. Slice the beef into bite-sized pieces.
2. Soak the beef for 15 minutes in a mixture of all the remaining ingredients, except the cooking oil.
3. Heat a frying-pan over a strong flame with the cooking oil and fry the beef until it changes colour. Remove from the pan and serve either hot or cold.

Stir-fried Beef with Leek

TSUNG CHAO NIU JOU

Preparation time : 25 minutes   Cooking time : 15 minutes

340g (12oz) beef
1 tablespoon Chinese wine or
*   dry sherry*
½ egg white
2 teaspoons cornflour

4 tablespoons oil
2 tablespoons bean paste*
4 tablespoons water
170g (6oz) leek
2 teaspoons sesame oil

1. Slice the beef thinly against the grain; then strip.
2. Mix the beef with the wine, egg white and cornflour.
3. Dissolve the bean paste in 4 tablespoons water.
4. Shred the leek thinly; place two-thirds on a platter.
5. Heat 4 tablespoons oil and stir-fry the beef over a high heat until tender. Stir in the bean paste mixture, followed by 2 teaspoons sesame oil. Remove from the pan and arrange on top of the leek. Sprinkle the remaining shredded leek over the surface.

   * *Bean paste can be substituted with Hoisin Sauce or 3 tablespoons soy sauce. Bean paste is made from soy beans and is salty* *and thick. It is used to flavour food and is sold in a can or packet. Hoisin Sauce is a thick, brownish red soy bean sauce with spice; it is sweet and spicy.*

Pearl Balls

CHEN CHU JOU WON

Preparation time : about 3 hours   Cooking time : 30 minutes

450g (1lb) minced beef
225g (8oz) potatoes
2 eggs
½ onion, chopped
1 teaspoon sugar

2 teaspoons soy sauce
2 teaspoons root ginger
2 teaspoons salt
2 cups glutinous rice*

1. Soak the rice for 3 hours or overnight.
2. Boil the potatoes until soft and mash. Leftover potatoes or instant potato mix may be used.
3. Finely chop the onion and ginger.
4. Mix the minced beef, mashed potato, eggs, onion and ginger together thoroughly. Add all the remaining ingredients, except the rice, and mix well again.
5. Using a tablespoon, shape the mixture into small balls.
6. Drain the soaked rice thoroughly and spread on a plate or tray. Roll the meat balls in the rice until they are well coated.
7. Place the meat balls in a steamer on a wet cheese cloth, or sit them in a pan of water and cover with a lid. Allow 1cm (½in) space between the meat balls to allow for the expansion of the rice.
8. Steam for 30 minutes. Serve hot.

Note : Mustard and soy sauce, served in separate dishes, can be provided as a dip for the pearl balls.

* Glutinous rice may be substituted with short grain rice.

Steamed Meat Roll

CHENG JOU JUEN

Preparation time : 15 minutes   Cooking time : 20 minutes

450g (1lb) minced meat
½ cup chopped onion or leek
1 tablespoon Chinese wine or
  dry sherry
½ teaspoon minced garlic
4 eggs
2 tablespoons cornflour

3 tablespoons oil
salt

Condiments
soy sauce
mustard

1. Mix the minced meat well with the chopped onion or leek, wine, a teaspoon salt, garlic, 1 egg, and the cornflour.
2. Heat the oil, scramble 3 eggs and remove to a plate.
3. Spread the minced meat on a large piece of greaseproof paper, place the scrambled egg on top of the meat sheet. Roll and place on a plate. Steam for 15 minutes.
4. Cut into pieces and serve with the cut edge on top. It will look like a jelly or swiss roll. Use the soy sauce and mustard as dips.

Deep-fried Liver with Curry

SHA ZU KAN

Preparation time : 15 minutes   Cooking time : 15 minutes

450g (1lb) pig's or calf's liver
2 teaspoons curry powder
3 tablespoons flour
1 egg

½ teaspoon salt
a little sugar
oil for deep-frying

1. Wash the liver, cut into finger-sized strips. Soak in water for 15 minutes, then drain.
2. Beat the egg with the curry powder, flour and salt. Add the liver and mix well.

3. Heat the oil and deep-fry the coated liver pieces until the colour changes. Serve.

Sauté Liver with Vegetables

CHAO KAN

Preparation time : 15 minutes   Cooking time : 5 minutes

225g (8oz) beef or pork liver	*1 clove garlic*
3 teaspoons Chinese wine or	*oil for deep-frying*
dry sherry	*3 tablespoons oil*
2 tablespoons cornflour	*1 tablespoon soy sauce*
½ onion	*½ teaspoon sugar*
1 green pepper	*½ teaspoon salt*

1. Cut the liver into bite-sized pieces and soak in water for 10 minutes. Dip into boiling water and drain at once.
2. Sprinkle with 2 teaspoons wine and the cornflour.
3. Measure the seasonings into a bowl.
4. Heat some oil; deep-fry the liver until it changes colour.
5. Cut the onion into 8 portions or bite-sized pieces.
6. Cut the green pepper into halves; remove the seeds and cut into bite-sized pieces.
7. Heat 3 tablespoons oil and sauté the garlic, onion, and green pepper for 2 minutes; add the deep-fried liver, soy sauce, sugar, and 1 teaspoon wine. Stir quickly and serve.

Genghis Khan Mutton

GENGHIS KHAN KAO YANG JOU

Preparation and cooking time : 30 minutes

450g (1lb) boneless mutton, leg or shoulder	Seasonings
	1 cup leek or scallions
2 pacific prawns	3 tablespoons grated garlic
10 mushrooms	½ cup Chinese wine or dry sherry
225g (8oz) spring onions	3 tablespoons chilli powder
2 peppers, 1 red and 1 green if possible	3 tablespoons ginger, chopped or grated
225g (8oz) spinach	½ cup coriander
1 onion	1 cup soy sauce
6 slices lemon	½ cup shrimp oil
1 piece of suet or a small amount of oil	½ cup sugar
	½ cup sesame oil

1. Slice the mutton thinly into bite-sized pieces.
2. Wash the prawns in running water, remove legs and devein.
3. Wash the vegetables thoroughly and drain. Cut the roots off the spring onions. Halve the peppers and remove the seeds. Peel and slice the round onion into circles – be careful that the pieces do not fall apart. Remove the stems from the mushrooms and wash quickly in salted water; wipe off the moisture.
4. Place the mutton, prawns and suet attractively on a platter. Set on the table.
5. Place the vegetables attractively on a large platter. Set on the table.
6. Place the seasonings in individual small bowls. Set on the table.
7. Heat the charcoal base of a Genghis Khan pan or barbecue grill. Place the grill over the charcoal and when it is very hot rub with the suet or a small amount of cooking oil to prevent sticking.
8. Each person helps to cook the pieces of food he prefers. He prepares the dip of the seasonings to his own taste. The food may be first dipped into the sauce, then placed upon the grill.

Alternatively the food may be dipped into the sauce after it has been cooked.

9. The meat, prawns and vegetables are placed in single layers on the grill and cooked on one side to a light brown. They are then turned and grilled on the other side. The grill has a rim around it to catch the juices as the food cooks. If such a pan is not available, a small bowl or plate may be used.

Notes : The meat may be sliced more thickly if it is cooked on the grill first, and then dipped into the mixed seasonings.

The Genghis Khan pan is a special pan made of iron which comes from the northern part of China. It is mainly used for cooking mutton. Another type, the Mongolian Grill, is also used for cooking at the table. Ideally, pinewood charcoal is required for fuel. The grill should be cleaned between each use. Wash and remove any bits of food clinging to the grill. Dry it very well and apply a thin coating of oil to the top surface to prevent rust.

Pork

Barbecued Pork Strips

KAO CHU DOU

Preparation time : 2–5 hours   *Cooking time : 40 minutes or*
1 hour 10 minutes

1kg (2¼lb) lean pork, pork
  shoulder or loin
1 teaspoon salt
1 teaspoon Five Spices
1 tablespoon honey
5 tablespoons soy sauce
2 tablespoons Chinese wine or
  dry sherry

1 tablespoon Hoisin Sauce or soy
  bean paste
½ cup chopped leek
3 slices ginger
1 tablespoon coarsely ground
  pepper
5 cloves aniseed

1. Cut meat into strips 5cm (2in) wide, 5cm (2in) thick and 15cm (6in) long. Bind each tightly with string.

2. Pierce the meat in several places with a knife, fork or skewer. Rub the meat with salt and Five Spices and place in a marinade made of the remaining ingredients except the sesame oil and honey. Marinate for 2–5 hours, turning the meat frequently.

3. Heat oven to 220C/425F/Mark 7. Grease a rack with oil to prevent the meat from sticking. Place pork strips on the rack over a roaster containing water. Barbecue meat for 30 minutes, reduce heat to 190C/375F/Mark 5. Remove from the oven. Cut into bite-sized pieces. Serve with plum sauce, mustard or soy sauce.

4. Another way to cook the meat is to place the pork strips in sufficient water to barely cover them and then add the marinade sauce to the water. Bring to a boil and simmer over a medium heat for 1 hour. Remove the meat from the liquid and wipe dry. Fry in deep oil until golden brown, then slice and serve.

Note : This pork is particularly delicious cooked on a charcoal grill.

Barbecued Pork Strips may be used in any meal and can be eaten either hot or cold. They can, for instance, be served on top of noodles; combined with a cold vegetable dish; or used for sandwiches on picnics.

Prepare in quantity and refrigerate for up to one week or wrap in foil and deep freeze.

Barbecued Spare Ribs

KAO PAL KU

Preparation time : 1 hour   Cooking time : 20 minutes

1kg (2¼lb) pork spare ribs   *2 tablespoons soy sauce**
2 tablespoons Chinese wine or   *1 tablespoon grated garlic*
dry sherry   *1 teaspoon salt*

1. Marinate the spare ribs with the wine, soy sauce, garlic and salt for 1 hour.
2. Preheat oven to 230C/450F/Mark 8; place marinated spare ribs in a roasting pan. Bake for 20 minutes or until golden brown. Cut ribs apart and serve.

   * *Bottled or canned Hoisin Sauce may be used as an alternative to soy sauce.*

Broiled Pork Loin

KAO CHU PAI

Preparation and cooking time : 25 minutes

4 pieces pork loin   *1 teaspoon minced garlic*
2 tablespoons soy sauce   *1 teaspoon minced ginger root*
1 tablespoon Chinese wine or   *(optional)*
dry sherry   *½ cup chopped onion*

1. Soak the pork with all the ingredients for about 5 minutes.
2. Place on rack and broil or grill for 20 minutes or until tender.
3. Cut into bite-sized pieces before serving.

Broiled Spare Ribs

KAO PAI KU

Preparation time : 3–4 hours   Cooking time : 30 minutes

2¼kg (about 5lb) pork spare ribs   1 tablespoon sugar
2 cups soy sauce   1 teaspoon minced garlic
½ cup Chinese wine or dry sherry

1. Clean and separate the ribs into 5cm (2in) lengths or longer.
2. Place the ribs in a bowl with the other ingredients. Turning them occasionally, marinate for 3–4 hours.
3. Broil on a broiler or grill for 30 minutes.

Fried Meat Pie

CHAO HO TZU

Preparation time : 30 minutes   Cooking time : 10 minutes

170g (6oz) finely minced pork or   1 tablespoon Chinese wine or
  beef   dry sherry
110g (4oz) spring onions or   2 hard boiled eggs
  celery   2 cups plain flour
3 tablespoons soy sauce   1 cup boiling water (vary
½ teaspoon salt   according to quality of flour)
2 tablespoons oil   oil for deep-frying

1. Heat 2 tablespoons oil in a frying-pan; stir-fry the minced meat and add the soy sauce, salt, and wine. Remove to a bowl.
2. Wash the spring onions or celery and chop them finely; cut the hard boiled eggs into small cubes.
3. Add the vegetables and egg to the meat and mix thoroughly.
4. Mix the flour with boiling water and knead into a soft dough. Cover with a damp cloth and allow to stand for 10 minutes or more before using.
5. Roll the dough on a board into a long sausage, and cut into pieces about the size of a golf ball.

6. Sprinkle the board with flour and flatten each ball into a thin pancake shape.
8. Place 1 tablespoon filling mixture between 2 pancake-shaped pieces and pinch the edges together.
9. Heat some oil and deep-fry the meat pies until light brown. Serve with soy sauce and vinegar.

Fried Sliced Pork in Batter

CHA JOU PIEN

Preparation time : 15 minutes   Cooking time : 15–20 minutes

450g (1lb) pork fillet
2 tablespoons Chinese wine or
   dry sherry
2 tablespoons soy sauce
oil for deep-frying

Batter
1 egg white
2 tablespoons chopped leek,
   onion or spring onions
2 tablespoons cornflour
4–5 tablespoons plain flour

1. Cut the meat into 20 cubes. Marinate in soy sauce and wine for 5 minutes.
2. Beat the egg white lightly. Mix with the rest of the batter ingredients.
3. Add the meat to the batter and mix well.
4. Heat the oil and deep-fry the meat until golden brown over a medium heat. The meat will be raw inside and burned outside if the heat is too strong.

Stir-fried Pork with Spring Onions

CHAO JOU SSU GU TSAI

Preparation and cooking time : 15 minutes

225g (8oz) pork, shredded
2 tablespoons soy sauce
1 tablespoon Chinese wine or
   dry sherry

225g (8oz) spring onions
5 tablespoons oil
½ teaspoon salt

1. Slice the pork very thinly against the grain, then shred it finely.
2. Dredge the shredded pork with the soy sauce and wine.
3. Wash the spring onions and cut into 5cm (2in) lengths, including green tops.
4. Heat the oil and sauté the pork. When the pork changes colour, add the spring onions and salt. Mix well and remove from heat before spring onions begin to lose their juices. Serve hot.

Note : Cabbage, celery, or bamboo shoots may be substituted for spring onions.

Fried Meatballs

CHA JOU WON

Preparation and cooking time : 30 minutes

450g (1lb) minced pork	1 tablespoon sesame oil
3 tablespoons chopped leek	2 tablespoons cornflour
½ teaspoon grated garlic	2 tablespoons flour
½ tablespoon ginger juice	oil for deep-frying
1 egg	
1 tablespoon Chinese wine or	Condiments
dry sherry	salt and black pepper
1 tablespoon soy sauce	sweet and pungent sauce

1. Mix all the ingredients together. Using a tablespoon, make the mixture into walnut-sized small balls, taking care not to over-handle or pack too tightly otherwise they will harden while cooking.
2. Heat the oil to 180C/350F and deep-fry the meatballs. Cook several at once, turning frequently for an even colour. When the meatballs float, remove from oil.
3. Before serving, reheat the oil and return the meatballs to the hot oil; fry for one minute until golden brown. Drain on absorbent paper. Arrange the meatballs on a serving plate. Serve with black pepper and salt or sweet and pungent sauce.

Sweet Meatballs

JOU WON

Preparation time : 20 minutes   Cooking time : 10 minutes

¼ cup (about 10) water chestnuts
   (canned) or ¼ cup celery,
   chopped
450g (1lb) minced pork
1 tablespoon chopped leek
½ teaspoon ginger juice
½ teaspoon garlic
1 egg
1 tablespoon Chinese wine or
   dry sherry
1 teaspoon salt
1 tablespoon soy sauce
1 tablespoon sesame seed oil
2 tablespoons flour
2 tablespoons cornflour

oil for deep-frying
20 Brussels sprouts
a dash of salt

Sauce
4 tablespoons sugar
4 tablespoons vinegar
2 tablespoons soy sauce
½ teaspoon salt
1 teaspoon Chinese wine or
   dry sherry
⅓ cup broth or water
1½ tablespoons cornflour
1½ cups water

1. Mix the first 12 ingredients well and, using a tablespoon, shape the mixture into small balls. Heat the oil to 180C/350F and deep-fry the meatballs over a medium heat until golden brown; the meatballs will float when ready.
2. Boil the Brussels sprouts with a dash of salt for about 8 minutes or until tender; drain.
3. Mix the cornflour and water for the sauce and put the rest of the ingredients in a pan; bring to the boil, stirring constantly. Thicken with the cornflour mixture then add the fried meatballs and Brussels sprouts. Serve hot.

Sweet and Sour Pork

TANG TSU JOU

Preparation and cooking time : 25 minutes

450g (1lb) lean pork
1 tablespoon Chinese wine or
  dry sherry
1 tablespoon soy sauce
1 egg, lightly beaten
1 tablespoon cornflour
3 tablespoons plain flour
3 slices canned pineapple drained
  and quartered, or use 1 cup
  pineapple chunks
oil for deep-frying

Sauce
1 small onion, quartered

3 green peppers, seeded and
  quartered (makes 2 cups)
1 clove garlic minced
3 tablespoons oil
$\frac{1}{3}$ cup sugar
4 tablespoons tomato sauce
1 tablespoon Chinese wine or
  dry sherry
2 tablespoons vinegar
2 tablespoons soy sauce mixed
  well with 1 tablespoon
  cornflour and $\frac{1}{2}$ cup water

1. Cut the meat into 4cm (1$\frac{1}{2}$in) cubes.
2. Mix the pork with wine, soy sauce, egg, cornflour and plain flour.
3. Heat the oil for deep-frying to 180C/350F. Separate pork pieces and deep-fry until well done and crisp on the edges. Remove to oven-proof platter that has been covered with absorbent paper and place in a low oven to keep warm.
4. Sauce: heat 3 tablespoons oil and sauté the garlic. When it becomes fragrant add the onion and green peppers and cook over a high heat for 2 minutes. Add the sugar, tomato sauce, wine and vinegar and the cornflour mixture. Bring to boiling point stirring constantly.
5. Add deep-fried pork and pineapple chunks, mix well and serve hot.

Sweet and Sour Pork with Fruits

TANG TSU KUO TZU JOU

Preparation time : 35 minutes   Cooking time : 10 minutes

*340g (12oz) pork or lean chuck
  steak
1 tablespoon soy sauce
1 tablespoon Chinese wine or
  dry sherry
2 tablespoons cornflour
1 egg
2–3 tablespoons plain flour
oil for deep-frying
1 cup pineapple slices
½ cup snow peas
3 tablespoons salad oil*

*(A)
½ cup broth or water
2 tablespoons pineapple
  syrup
½ teaspoon salt
1 tablespoon soy sauce
1 tablespoon cornflour
3 tablespoons water
2 tablespoons sugar
1 tablespoon Chinese wine or
  dry sherry*

1. Cut the pork into chunks and marinate with soy sauce and wine for 5 minutes, then mix in the cornflour.
2. Beat the egg and plain flour together to make a batter.
3. Cut each pineapple slice into 6 pieces.
4. Remove strings from the snow peas.
5. Mix all ingredients (*A*) into a bowl.
6. Dip the pork into the batter and deep-fry until golden brown.
7. Fry the snow peas in 3 tablespoons oil. Add the pineapple, fried pork, and ingredients (*A*) and mix well. Simmer until the sauce thickens.

Roast Dumpling

KUO TE

Preparation and cooking time : 1 hour and 20 minutes

Filling
110g (4oz) minced pork
140g (5oz) cabbage
½ cup finely chopped leek
*½ teaspoon finely chopped
    ginger*
*1 tablespoon Chinese wine or
    dry sherry*
1½ tablespoons soy sauce
⅓ teaspoon salt
1½ tablespoons sesame oil
2 tablespoons oil

Dumpling Wrappers
1½ cups flour
*½ cup boiling water (may need
    more water according to the
    quality of the flour)*
½ cup flour for the rolling board

Condiments
soy sauce
vinegar
fermented soy bean paste (optional)
chilli sauce
grated garlic

1. Shred the cabbage and drop it into boiling water for 2
minutes. Rinse with cold water and drain well. Chop the
cabbage very finely. Place it in the corner of a tea towel, or
cheese cloth, and squeeze out the moisture.
2. In a bowl combine the pork, cabbage, leek, ginger root, salt,
wine, soy sauce, and sesame oil and mix very well. Set aside.
3. Sift the flour into another bowl. Pour the boiling water into
the flour and stir briskly. Add more water, a few drops at a
time, to make a firm yet pliable dough. Mix the dough with
chopsticks, or a fork, until it is cool enough to put your hands
on. Then press it into a smooth ball – the Chinese say until it
is the softness of the ear lobe.
4. Turn the dough out onto a lightly floured board and knead
it thoroughly and firmly by hand until it is satin-smooth and
elastic. Transfer it to a bowl, cover with a damp cloth, and let
the dough stand 20–25 minutes.
5. Place the dough on lightly floured board. Knead briefly
once again.
6. Holding the dough with both hands, shape into a cylinder
about 4cm (1½in) in diameter.

7. Cut the cylinder into two pieces, and divide each half into 6 pieces to make 12 sections.

8. Sprinkle each piece lightly with flour. Roll a piece into a ball. Then, with your palm, flatten the roll into a circle about 10cm (4in) in diameter. A rolling pin may be used, but the centre of the circle should be a little thicker than the edges. Repeat with the remaining 11 pieces.

9. Hold a wrapper in the left hand. Place 1/12th of the filling in the centre of the wrapper and slightly flatten it with chopsticks or a fork.

10. Fold the wrapper in half to make a half moon shape and pinch the edges together at the top centre of the arc.

11. Pinch the right end of the half moon by thumb and index finger to seal.

12. Then make a small pleat on the back side of the wrapper, press it to the right and seal it to the side facing you. Repeat on the left side. Make the other 11 dumplings in the same manner. Be sure that the edges are completely sealed.

13. To cook the dumplings: place 2 tablespoons oil in a flat-bottomed frying-pan which has a lid to fit it and heat over a medium heat. Hold the dumplings by the sealed edge and place them in a line, smooth side down, in the hot pan. Cook, without the lid, for 1 or 2 minutes until the dumplings are brown and appear firm, or crispy. Pour $\frac{1}{2}$ cup hot water into the pan and cover with the lid. Cook about 3 minutes until the water has evaporated. Remove the dumplings from the pan and serve browned side up.

14. Serve with condiments. Each person mixes the condiments to his own taste, or one premixed bowl of condiments may be served.

Tung Po Pork

TUNG PO JOU

Advanced cooking time : 2 hours 40 minutes   Cooking time before serving : 20 minutes

450g (1lb) fresh bacon, cut in one piece with skin on	*3 tablespoons oil*
	1 teaspoon sugar
25cm (10in) leek	*2 cloves star aniseed*
4 slices ginger root	*1 teaspoon cornflour*
2 tablespoons Chinese wine or dry sherry	*225g (8oz) spinach*
	½ teaspoon salt
2½ tablespoons soy sauce	

1. Cut the bacon into 4cm (1½in) sections, being very careful to keep the skin intact. The skin should remain in one piece. Cut the leek into 2 or 3 sections. Slice the ginger root.
2. Place the meat in a pan; add the leek, ginger, 1 tablespoon of wine, and enough water to cover the meat. Bring to the boil. Simmer over a medium heat for one hour or until tender. (A pressure cooker may be used at this point.) Drain.
3. Soak the skin side of the meat in 1 tablespoon of soy sauce for five minutes or more to colour the skin. Heat 1 tablespoon oil in a pan over a medium heat and fry the top, bottom and sides, particularly the top of the pork, until golden brown.
4. Cut through the skin to make separate cubes of pork.
5. Place the pork in a bowl with the fat side down and sprinkle with the sugar, 1½ tablespoons soy sauce, 1 tablespoon wine and the aniseed. Steam over a medium heat for about one hour.
6. Drain the liquid, about ½ cup, from steamed pork, and let it cool a little; add the cornflour and boil until it thickens. Set aside.
7. Wash the spinach thoroughly. Do not discard the ends and stems but slice them into strips.
8. Heat 2 tablespoons oil; add the spinach and salt and stir-fry until just tender.
9. Place the hot pork, skin side up, in the centre of a serving plate. Arrange the hot spinach around it.

10. Pour the thickened sauce over the pork and spinach. Serve hot.

Note : This dish was a favourite of Soo-Tung-Po a well-known poet of the Tang Dynasty. The pork should be cooked until very tender ; it should melt in your mouth.

Step 2. The broth from the meat may be strained, the grease skimmed off the top, and used for stock in another recipe.

The steaming in Step 5 can be done in two stages. Steam first for 30 minutes. Steam another 30 minutes just before serving.

Chilled Kidney

LIANG PAN YAO HUA

Preparation time : 2 hours 20 minutes   Cooking time : 10 minutes

2 kidneys
3 slices of ginger
2 tablespoons Chinese wine or
  dry sherry

Peppercorn Sauce
1 teaspoon ground black
  peppercorns
1 tablespoon sesame oil
2 tablespoons soy sauce
2 tablespoons broth
1 tablespoon Chinese wine or
  dry sherry

Sesame Sauce
3 tablespoons sesame paste*
1 teaspoon salt
3 tablespoons water
1 tablespoon mustard
½ tablespoon vinegar

Garlic Sauce
2 tablespoons sesame oil
2 tablespoons soy sauce
1 teaspoon minced garlic
1 teaspoon ginger
½ teaspoon sugar

1. Cut the kidneys in half lengthwise and remove all the white membrane.
2. Soak the kidneys in salted water for at least 2 hours.
3. Score each piece on the top side in a criss-cross pattern, then cut into bite-sized pieces.
4. Bring to the boil in sufficient water to cover, with wine and

ginger, and cook for about 5 minutes – kidney will easily harden if overcooked. Rinse with cold water, drain, and place on a serving platter.
5. Mix the various sauces in separate bowls and serve with the kidney.

* *Sesame paste may be substituted with peanut butter.*

Poultry

Braised Chicken Legs

HUNG SHAO CHI CHIAO

Preparation time : 35 minutes *Cooking time : 25 minutes*

4 chicken legs
3 tablespoons soy sauce
2 tablespoons Chinese wine or
   dry sherry
½ teaspoon grated ginger

2 tablespoons oil
2 tablespoons sesame seeds
2 slices pineapple or 4 water
   chestnuts

1. Wash the chicken legs; soak in soy sauce, wine and grated ginger for 30 minutes.

2. Heat the oil; stir-fry the chicken legs until the colour changes, turning constantly to make sure the colour turns light brown evenly.

3. Add the sauce left over from soaking the chicken legs. Cover with a tight-fitting lid and cook until tender – about 20 minutes.

4. Toast the sesame seeds in an ungreased frying pan until they pop. Sprinkle over the top of the chicken and serve with pineapple or water chestnuts.

Stewed Chicken with Taro Root

HUNG SHAO YU TO CHI

Preparation time : 20 minutes   Cooking time : 40 minutes

1 spring chicken, about
  1kg (2¼lb)
450g (1lb) taro root
¼ of a leek, finely sliced
3 slices ginger
3 tablespoons oil

oil for deep-frying
6 tablespoons soy sauce
3 tablespoons Chinese wine or
  dry sherry
1 tablespoon sugar
1 cup water

1. Joint and chop the chicken into 5cm (2in) sections. Wash and wipe dry. Marinate in 2 tablespoons wine and 2 tablespoons soy sauce for 20 minutes.

2. Heat 3 tablespoons oil in pan. First add the leek and ginger and cook for 30 seconds. Add the chicken and stir-fry until the chicken pieces become nicely browned. Then add the remaining soy sauce and wine, sugar and water. Turn the heat to low and cover the pan with a lid. Simmer for 20 minutes.

3. Peel the taro root and cut into chunks. Heat the oil and deep-fry the taro root until golden brown. Add to the chicken and cook together for 15 minutes. Serve hot.

Note : Fat may be removed from the chicken. Cut the fat into cubes and melt it in the pan to use as a substitute for the oil.

Deep-fried Crisp Chicken

TSUI PI CHI

Preparation time : 40 minutes   Cooking time : 20 minutes

450g (1lb) spring chicken
½ leek
1 teaspoon black pepper
2 teaspoons ginger juice or
 minced ginger
2 tablespoons Chinese wine or
 dry sherry

4 tablespoons cornflour
3 tablespoons soy sauce
oil for deep-frying

Condiment
salt and pepper mixture

1. Cut the chicken into 4cm (1½in) cubes; wash thoroughly.
2. Chop the leek into small sections.
3. Marinate the chicken cubes with wine, soy sauce, pepper and ginger juice for 30 minutes. Stir the mixture from time to time.
4. Mix the chicken cubes with cornflour.
5. Heat the oil, add the chicken a few pieces at a time and deep-fry until light golden brown. Remove from the oil and drain. Fry once again to make more crisp.
6. Drain on paper towels and serve with the condiment.

Note : There are many different ways to deep-fry chicken : whole, boned, jointed or cubed ; marinate first, then deep-fry plain or coated with batter.

Deep-fried Chicken with Peking Sauce

YOU LIN CHI

Preparation time : 1 hour   Cooking time : 40 minutes

1 spring chicken (about
    1 kg/2¼lb)
3 tablespoons Chinese wine or
    dry sherry
6 tablespoons soy sauce
12½cm (5in) leek
3 slices ginger
oil for deep-frying

Sauce
3 tablespoons soy sauce
1 tablespoon vinegar
1 tablespoon sesame oil
½ tablespoon sugar
¼ cup chopped leek
1 teaspoon ginger chopped
½ teaspoon minced garlic
water

1. Clean the chicken, and remove the hair carefully with tweezers. Halve the chicken with a cleaver or knife; dry with a paper towel.
2. Cut the leek into 2½cm (1in) lengths; slice the ginger.
3. Place the chicken in a bowl and add the leek, ginger, soy sauce, and wine; soak for about one hour, turning occasionally.
4. Prepare the sauce in a small bowl.
5. Heat the oil; wipe the chicken with a paper towel. Deep-fry one half until golden brown. Keep pouring oil over the top of the chicken with a ladle.
6. Deep-fry the other half in the same way.
7. Chop the deep-fried chicken into 5cm (2in) sections and place on a platter.
8. Before serving pour the sauce over the top.

Note : Remove the big bone before chopping as it is then easier to cut.

Fried Chicken with Cashew Nuts

YAO KUO CHI TING

Preparation and cooking time : 20 minutes

340g (12oz) chicken meat
½ cup cashew nuts
½ egg white
1 teaspoon cornflour
10cm (4in) leek cut into
 1cm (½in) sections
1 slice ginger
oil for deep-frying
1½ teaspoons cornflour
1½ tablespoons water

Seasoning
1½ teaspoons Chinese wine or
 dry sherry
½ teaspoon salt
1 tablespoon soy sauce
½ teaspoon sugar

1. Skin and bone the chicken. Cut the chicken into slices on the bias about 1cm (½in) thick. Cut into cubes; cube on the bias to make the edges thinner.
2. Mix the chicken cubes with egg white and cornflour.
3. Heat the oil to 160C/320F and deep-fry the cashew nuts, stirring constantly until golden brown. Nuts burn easily, so as soon as the colour changes remove from the pan and drain.
4. Heat 6 tablespoons oil and sauté the ginger and leek with the chicken until the chicken changes colour. Add seasoning, toss for about 30 seconds to mix well. Add the cornflour and water mixed together and cook for about 30 seconds more, stirring constantly. Add cashew nuts, mix thoroughly and serve hot.

Note : Stir-fried chicken requires a very short cooking time. This dish is often made using a combination of vegetables, or nuts and vegetables.

Dark meat and white meat may be used, however, all white meat is preferable.

Save the skin and bones to use in making stock. Most Chinese like to keep the skin on the meat as they enjoy the flavour.

Fried Chicken and Glutinous Rice Balls

CHA NO MI CHI CHUO

Preparation time : 1 hour   Cooking time : 15 minutes

1½ cups glutinous rice
1½ cups water or more
2 tablespoons soy sauce
oil for deep-frying

(A)
200g (7oz) minced chicken
½ teaspoon ginger juice
¼ teaspoon salt
1 egg
3 tablespoons chopped bamboo
   shoots
2 tablespoons chopped mushrooms

(B)
2 eggs
5 tablespoons flour
2 tablespoons water
½ teaspoon salt
dash of black pepper
½ teaspoon baking powder
1 tablespoon lard

1. Wash the rice; add 1½ cups water and bring to the boil. Turn to a low heat, and simmer for 20 minutes, or until water has evaporated. Turn off the heat, and allow to stand for 10 minutes. Add soy sauce and mix well.
2. Divide into 24 patties.
3. Mix ingredients (A) and form them into 24 patties to fit on top of the rice. Place one meat patty on top of each rice patty. Press firmly together to form round balls.
4. Mix ingredients (B) for batter.
5. Dip the balls in the batter and deep-fry until golden brown in hot oil.

Note : Fried chicken and glutinous rice balls can be cooked in advance and reheated in an oven before serving. Short grain rice can be substituted for glutinous rice. According to the quality of the rice the amount of water needed will vary so it is best to read the packet instructions.

Fried Chicken Wrapped in Paper

CHIH BO CHI

Preparation time : 25 minutes Cooking time : 7 minutes

225g (8oz) chicken or beef
2 tablespoons soy sauce
1 tablespoon Chinese wine or
 dry sherry
12 slices ginger
1 teaspoon curry powder
 (optional)
12 slices ham

12 snow peas
12 slices mushroom
2 teaspoons sesame oil (or salad
 oil)
oil for deep-frying
12 squares of greaseproof or
 cellophane paper (15cm/6in)

1. Cut the chicken into 4cm (1½in) cubes or slice the beef into bite-sized pieces.
2. Combine the soy sauce and wine; marinate the meat for 10 minutes.
3. Fold each square of greaseproof paper like an envelope, then open them up.
4. Brush the sesame oil or salad oil in the centre of the paper squares. Place a piece of meat on each, and also a slice each of ginger, ham, mushroom, curry powder and a snow pea.
5. Fold the paper envelopes and tuck in the flap securely.
6. Heat the oil to 180C/350F and deep-fry, flap-side up, until golden brown. Drain on a paper towel. To eat, break the centre of the paper with a chopstick or fork.

Sweet and Sour Chicken

TANG TSU CHI

Preparation time : 10 minutes Cooking time : 20 minutes

450g (1lb) chicken meat
2 tablespoons Chinese wine or
 dry sherry
3 tablespoons cornflour
oil for deep-frying

1 cup sliced apple
1 tablespoon soy sauce
3 tablespoons vinegar
5 tablespoons sugar
1 cup water or broth

1. Bone the chicken, cut into bite-sized pieces, and mix with the wine and 2 tablespoons cornflour.
2. Heat the oil; deep-fry the chicken until golden brown, and arrange on a platter.
3. Boil all the seasonings with the water or broth and 1 table-spoon cornflour; stir constantly until thickened.
4. Add the sliced apple and fried chicken pieces to the sauce. Serve.

Shredded Chicken with Glass Vermicelli

CHI SSU LA PI

Preparation time and cooking time : 40 minutes

110g (4oz) chicken meat
225g (8oz) cucumber

Glass vermicelli
¾ cup cornflour or green bean starch or lotus powder
½ cup water

Sauce
2 tablespoons sesame paste*
4 tablespoons water
1 tablespoon vinegar
2 tablespoons soy sauce

1. Boil a spring chicken for 30 minutes or a 'boiling' chicken for 1 hour. Remove the bones and shred meat.
2. Clean the cucumber; slice and shred.
3. Cut glass vermicelli (see method for making below) 1cm (½in) wide and 10cm (4in) long and soak in cold water.
4. Mix the sesame paste with water, adding the water gradually until the paste becomes very smooth. Add the vinegar and soy sauce.
5. Drain the glass vermicelli and arrange in a circle on the serving plate. Place the cucumber and chicken in the centre and pour over the sauce.

Glass Vermicelli
Mix the cornflour and water in a bowl. Into a small skillet placed over boiling water, drop 2 tablespoons of vermicelli batter. Turn skillet to spread the batter evenly and allow to

cook until firm (about 2 minutes). Immediately put the skillet over cold water and when the vermicelli is cool, remove from pan. Place the vermicelli in a bowl of cold water until ready to use. Repeat process.

* Sesame paste may be substituted with peanut butter.
Use chicken with skin. Skin increases the flavour. This is a cold dish and should be prepared in advance. Keep the sauce in a separate dish until serving.

White Cut Cold Chicken

PAI CHIEH CHI

Preparation time : 15 minutes   Cooking time : 30 minutes

1 spring chicken	2 teaspoons sesame oil
1 leek	2 teaspoons Chinese wine or
1 star aniseed (optional)	dry sherry
1 tablespoon black peppercorns	¾ teaspoon salt
(optional)	2 teaspoons soy sauce
4 slices ginger	

1. Clean chicken and cut the leek into 5cm (2in) lengths.
2. Place aniseed and peppercorns in a small cloth bag, so that they can be easily discarded after use.
3. Place chicken, leek, spices and ginger in a pot with enough water to half-cover the chicken. Cover and bring to the boil. Lower heat, move lid slightly to allow steam to escape and simmer for 30 minutes.
4. Remove the chicken and rinse it under cold running water to make the skin firm and smooth. Dry with a cloth.
5. Brush with sesame oil and rub with wine and salt.
6. Bone and slice.
7. Sprinkle with soy sauce and sesame oil to taste. Serve cold.

Note : The chicken may also be cooked by placing it in a deep heat-proof dish. Place the dish in a steamer and steam for 30–40 minutes. Save the juices for a soup ; they are as good for this purpose as when the chicken is boiled. Chicken skin can be re-

moved. However there is a fine layer of fat beneath the skin, which after it is cooked becomes fine and satiny. It is therefore better to leave the skin on to enjoy the delicate taste and flavour.

Sauté Chicken Liver

CHAO CHI KAN

Preparation time : 30 minutes   Cooking time : 5 minutes

450g (1lb) chicken liver
4 tablespoons soy sauce
2 tablespoons Chinese wine or
  dry sherry
1 tablespoon sugar

½ cup leek or onion chopped
1 teaspoon fresh ginger or
  ginger powder
4 tablespoons sesame oil

1. Clean the chicken liver; cut into 4 or 5 pieces. Marinate with soy sauce, wine, sugar, leek, and grated ginger for about 20 minutes.
2. Remove the liver from the sauce. Drain the sauce and set aside.
3. Heat the sesame oil, sauté the liver. When the colour changes, add the drained sauce and stir until boiling. Serve either hot or cold.

Stir-fried Chicken Liver with Cucumber

CHAO CHI KAN

Preparation time : 20 minutes   Cooking time : 5 minutes

225g (8oz) chicken liver
1 small cucumber
1 clove garlic
1 stalk leek
1 tablespoon Chinese wine or
  dry sherry

3 tablespoons oil
1 teaspoon salt
1 teaspoon sugar
2 teaspoons cornflour
2 tablespoons water
1 tablespoon sesame oil

1. Slice the liver into 6 pieces and soak in water for 10 minutes; drain and boil in new water. Drain off the boiling water and wash the liver.
2. Cut the cucumber into pieces the same size as the liver.
3. Break the garlic with a heavy knife.
4. Slice the leek.
5. Heat the oil in a pan and add the garlic. When the colour changes discard the garlic. Add the leek and liver; stir-fry for a few minutes. Add the cucumber, wine and seasonings; thicken with a cornflour paste, stir well and serve.

Braised Duck

HUNG SHAO YA

Preparation time : 10 minutes   Cooking time : 35 minutes

1 duckling (about 1½kg/3lb)   *1 tablespoon sugar*
3 slices ginger   *3 tablespoons soy sauce*
2 cloves garlic   *1 cup water*
5 tablespoons oil   *1 tablespoon cornflour*
½ tablespoon star aniseed   *3 tablespoons water*

1. Cut the duck into 5cm (2in) cubes. Slice the ginger and crush the garlic.
2. Heat the oil. Stir-fry the garlic and ginger; when fragrant, add the duck cubes and stir-fry until brown.
3. Add the aniseed, sugar and soy sauce; stir, add water and bring to the boil. Turn down the flame and simmer until duck is tender – about 30 minutes.
4. Thicken with the cornflour mixed with the water. Serve with any vegetable dish or pineapple.

POULTRY souls...

Roast Duck

KAO YA

Cooking time : 1 hour 20 minutes

1 duck (2–2½kg/4–5½lb)	2 tablespoons soy sauce
1 teaspoon salt	1 tablespoon honey
3 teaspoons Chinese wine or	1 leek or onion (cut into sections)
dry sherry	3 slices ginger

1. Clean the duck; boil with the wine, and salt, and simmer for 15 minutes. Remove the duck from the pan; drain and rub with the soy sauce and honey. Stuff the leek and ginger into the cavity.
2. Heat the oven to 180C/350F/Mark 4. Place the duck on a rack over a dripping-pan containing water. Roast for 1 hour. Add more water to the dripping-pan if it evaporates. Serve with deep-fried nuts, e.g. cashew nuts.

Roast Peking Duck

PEKING KAO YA

Preparation time : 1½ days   Cooking time : 1 hour 10 minutes

1 duck (about 2kg/4½lb)	¼ teaspoon pepper
1 cup honey	2 tablespoons Chinese wine or
½ cup hot water	dry sherry
1 teaspoon salt	1 tablespoon vinegar

1. Boil plenty of water in a large pan. Put the duck in and remove as soon as the skin changes colour (50–60 minutes); drain.
2. Hang the duck to dry overnight or for one day in a cool and airy place.
3. Dissolve the honey in the hot water. Brush the honey all over the duck skin and dry. Repeat 2 or 3 times.
4. Rub salt and pepper in duck cavity. Hang the duck for a further half a day.

5. Rub the wine and vinegar in the duck cavity.

6. Heat the oven to 230C/450F/Mark 8. Place the duck on a rack over a dripping-pan containing water. Roast for 30 minutes; reduce heat to 120C/250F/Mark ½, and roast for 40 minutes more. Serve.

Note : There are many ways to cook duck in Chinese cooking, they can be steamed, braised, deep-fried, smoked, and roasted.

In Peking, there is a special way to raise ducks to make them very fat, and they are then inflated with air and roasted in a special stove to make the skin crisp. This is an imitation Peking Duck, and has a wonderful taste. When the legs of the duck move easily in their joints, the duck is ready.

Special Szechuan Smoked Duck

ZANG CHA YA

Preparation time : 11 hours and 30 minutes   Cooking time : 20 minutes

1 duck (about 2¼kg/5lb)	(A)
2 tablespoons salt	3 tablespoons salt
1 teaspoon kalium nitras- potassium (optional)	2 tablespoons star aniseed
	2 tablespoons peppercorns
water	1 stalk leek or 1 bunch scallions
1 cup wet tea leaves	3 tablespoons peppercorns
½ cup sawdust or pine tree	6 slices ginger
needles	2 tangerine peels

1. Clean the duck and season by rubbing with the salt and kalium mixture inside and outside and let stand for 3 hours.

2. Add ingredients (A) to some water and bring to the boil. Soak the duck in it for about 7 hours. Drain and dry; remove the fat from the duck.

3. Place some aluminium paper on the bottom of a pan with a lid, and place the wet tea leaves and sawdust or pine needles over it. Then place a rack over this and the duck on top. Cover

with paper (to keep the inside of the lid clean) and fit a lid tightly; smoke for 15–30 minutes.

4. Steam the smoked duck for one hour; lay it aside until cool and ready for use.

5. Before serving, deep-fry the duck in hot oil on each side until it turns golden brown. Cut into bite-sized pieces. Arrange on a platter.

6. Method of cutting: cut the wings and legs from the bird and cut them each into 4 sections, divide the body lengthwise into two and sidewise into 1cm ($\frac{1}{2}$in) wide pieces. The meat turns to a pink colour because of the seasoning with salt and kalium.

Fish

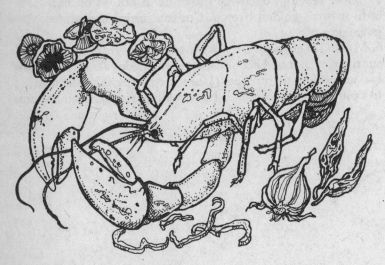

Braised Stuffed Abalone

HUNG SHAO PAO YU

Preparation time : 30 minutes   *Cooking time : 18 minutes*

1 can abalone (425g/15oz)
5 tablespoons oil
1 cup broth or water
2½ teaspoons salt
½ teaspoon sugar
2 teaspoons cornflour
2 tablespoons water
170g (6oz) lettuce (about 1 head)

Filling
60g (2oz) minced chicken
½ teaspoon salt

½ teaspoon Chinese wine or
dry sherry
a dash of pepper
1 egg white (keep yolk)
1 teaspoon cornflour

Batter
1 egg
1 egg yolk (from filling)
4 tablespoons flour
a dash of salt

1. Pull off the dark spongy part from the abalone.
2. Cut the abalone in half crosswise and split each piece in half again. There should be 24 pieces.
3. Make a pocket in each piece.
4. Mix the filling with a fork or chopsticks.
5. Stuff one teaspoonful filling in each pocket of abalone.
6. Mix the batter in a bowl.
7. Dip each piece of abalone into the batter.
8. Heat 3 tablespoons oil in a frying pan. Fry a few pieces at a time on both sides until golden brown. Remove to a plate.
9. Place the fried abalone in the pan again; add ½ teaspoon each of salt and sugar and the broth. Boil for 5 minutes. Add the cornflour mixed with 2 tablespoons water. Shake the pan to mix well. Serve hot.
10. Clean the lettuce; heat 2 tablespoons oil and fry the lettuce over a high flame for 2 minutes; add 2 teaspoons salt, and serve with abalone.

Note : Lettuce can be served raw if desired.

Steamed Abalone

CHENG PAO YU

Preparation time : 50 minutes   Cooking time : 20 minutes

1 can abalone (225g/8oz)   2 tablespoons Chinese wine or
450g (1lb) pork loin   dry sherry
1 leek or onion   a dash of black pepper
8 slices ginger   1½ tablespoons cornflour
¼ teaspoon salt   1 cup broth
2 tablespoons soy sauce

1. Boil the pork loin with half the leek and 4 slices of ginger for 40 minutes or until tender. Slice the meat and save the broth.
2. Slice the abalone and wash with boiling water.

3. Arrange the abalone and pork on a platter. Sprinkle over the wine and salt and steam with the other half stalk of leek and 4 slices of ginger for 15 minutes.
4. Heat 1 cup broth and the soy sauce, black pepper, and cornflour; stir until thickened and pour over the abalone and pork before serving.

Note : if dried abalone is used, boil it first for 3 hours and clean it with a brush.

Stir-fried Clams in Shells

CHAO HSIEH HSIA

Preparation time : 5 minutes   Cooking time : 7 minutes

24 clams	2 red chilli peppers (optional)
3 cloves garlic	4 tablespoons cooking oil
7½cm (3in) leek	2 tablespoons Chinese wine or
½ teaspoon salt	dry sherry

1. Wash the clams, brush the shell if necessary, remove sand under running water.
2. Mince the garlic and shred the leek.
3. Halve the red chilli peppers; remove seeds.
4. Heat the oil, add the garlic, leek, and red chilli peppers; when they become fragrant, add the clams, wine and salt and stir-fry.
5. Reduce the heat, cover, and when the shells open (about 7 minutes), serve; do not remove the shells.

Note : clams make a good soup too.

Deep-fried Crab Rolls

CHA HSIEH JUEN

Preparation and cooking time : 40 minutes

*110g (4oz) crab meat (canned,
  frozen or fresh)*
2 eggs
60g (2oz) bamboo shoots
1 leek
*1 dried mushroom or 5 button
  mushrooms*
60g (2oz) bean sprouts
3 tablespoons oil

½ teaspoon salt
1 teaspoon soy sauce
4 teaspoons flour
4 teaspoons water
oil for deep-frying

Condiments
tomato sauce
pepper and salt

1. Remove the soft bone (gristle) from the crab; separate the meat into bite-sized pieces.
2. Shred the bamboo shoots and leek.
3. Soak the dried mushroom in lukewarm water for 20 minutes until soft. Shred it into pieces the same size as the bamboo shoots and leek.
4. Wash the bean sprouts in running water, remove any black hulls and drain.
5. Heat the oil in a pan, stir-fry the leek rapidly, then add the mushrooms, bamboo shoots, bean sprouts, and cook, stirring constantly. Add ¼ teaspoon salt and 1 teaspoon soy sauce; mix 2 teaspoons cornflour with 2 teaspoons water and add to the pan, continue to stir until the mixture thickens. Transfer it to a plate and chill.
6. Mix 1 teaspoon cornflour with 1 teaspoon water in a bowl. Beat the eggs lightly with ¼ teaspoon salt and add to the corn-flour mixture; divide the mixture equally between 4 teacups or other containers.
7. Heat the pan thoroughly, rub with a little oil to cover the whole surface of the pan, including sides.
8. Pour the contents of one of the teacups, or other containers, into the pan, turn the pan around rapidly, and let the egg spread into a thin sheet 15cm (6in) in diameter.
9. Remove the egg sheet from the pan as soon as the edges are

dry. Remove from pan by turning pan upside down over a flat dish or peel egg sheet carefully from pan with fingers. Repeat the process 3 more times.

10. Mix 1 teaspoon flour with 1 teaspoon water to use for sealing the rolls. Put the thinly fried egg sheet on a chopping board. Place a quarter of the crab mixture on the lower half of the egg sheet.

11. Fold the bottom of the egg sheet up over the crab. Turn the left and right sides over the sides then roll. Moisten the top edges with the flour and water to seal.

12. Heat oil for deep-frying to 180C/350F in a pan and fry the rolls until golden brown. Cut into sections and serve with tomato sauce or pepper and salt.

Note : The egg sheets will be difficult to remove from the pan unless the oil is heated thoroughly before the mixture is added.

Since the bottom of the Chinese wok (pan) is not flat, the egg should be turned quickly around and from side to side otherwise it will get thick at the centre of the circle. It can be made thinner this way than in an ordinary frying-pan.

The filling can be varied with other ingredients.

Cuttle Fish with Cauliflower

TSAI HUA YOU YU

Preparation and cooking time : 20 minutes

1 cuttle fish or squid	1 clove garlic, crushed
½ teaspoon ginger juice	2 teaspoons cornflour
½ teaspoon cornflour	2 teaspoons water
½ cup peanuts	
oil for deep-frying	Seasonings
1 cup shrimps	½ cup water
1 teaspoon Chinese wine or	2 teaspoons soy sauce
dry sherry	2 teaspoons sugar
2 tablespoons oil	½ teaspoon salt
½ head cauliflower	1 tablespoon oil
vinegar	1 teaspoon sesame oil (optional)

1. Remove the legs and the intestine from the cuttle fish or squid. Open the meat out flat by cutting down the middle with a knife. Sprinkle the cuttle fish with salt to prevent it from being slippery. Remove the thin skin. Wash. Pat dry.

2. On one side of the cuttle fish score the flesh with a sharp knife in a diagonal design, or crosswise pattern. Be careful not to cut through the flesh. Cut the cuttle fish into bite-sized pieces about 4cm (1½in) by 5cm (2in) long.

3. Sprinkle with ginger juice and ½ teaspoon cornflour and parboil. Remove and soak in cold water.

4. Shell and de-vein shrimps. Sprinkle with wine and cornflour.

5. Cut off the tough end of the stem of the cauliflower. Remove the leaves, separate into flowerets. Parboil with a little vinegar in the water to help the colour stay white. When stalk is tender, drain.

6. Heat plenty of oil for deep-frying. Fry peanuts until golden brown. Drain.

7. Heat 2 tablespoons oil and add the garlic; when it becomes fragrant add the shrimps and stir-fry for about 30 seconds. When the colour changes, add cuttle fish or squid, cauliflower and seasonings. Then add the cornflour mixed with water and stir constantly until thickened. Add fried peanuts. Serve hot.

Bird's Nest Balls

CHÊNG YEN TSAI WON TZU

Preparation time : 30 minutes   Cooking time : 20 minutes

1½ cups prepared bird's nest*	*1 tablespoon cornflour*
340g (12oz) chicken meat	*½ teaspoon salt*
5 tablespoons water	*¼ teaspoon sugar*
2 teaspoons Chinese wine or	*1 egg white, lightly beaten*
dry sherry	

1. Soak the bird's nest overnight in cold water; remove any loose feathers with tweezers. Separate and clean; boil for 10

minutes. Rinse. If chips are used (see note), soak in boiling water then boil in fresh water for 30 minutes.

2. Mince the chicken meat and gradually add the water, wine, salt, sugar, cornflour and egg white. Form small balls with a tablespoon; roll in the separated bird's nest (which should look like transparent vermicelli), coating each ball evenly. Steam on a heat-proof plate in a steamer for 20 minutes.

 * *Whole bird's nest is the best quality and is shaped like a cup. However, dried bird's nest chips may be substituted. A bird's nest dish is one of the most expensive, delicate dishes and shows great hospitality at a formal dinner. The edible gelatinous saliva produced by tiny swallows in the South China Sea, which is beige in colour, looks like shredded glazed dried seaweed; it has a high content of proteins and vitamins. Ten centuries ago, Chinese ladies had bird's nest soup, or bird's nest with rock sugar, as a sweet tea, to keep a youthful complexion.*

Baked Fish

KAU YU

Preparation time : 15 minutes   Cooking time : 20 minutes

450g (1lb) fish (about 1 fish)   2 tablespoons Chinese wine or
2 tablespoons soy sauce   dry sherry
3 slices ginger   salt
2 tablespoons sugar

1. Clean and scale the fish; make 3 diagonal slashes on each side. Sprinkle with some wine and salt; let stand for 10 minutes.

2. Boil the wine, soy sauce, ginger and sugar until thickened or reduced to about half the quantity. Remove to a bowl.

3. Bake the fish in a moderate oven until half-cooked (about 15 minutes) then brush the boiled sauce on both sides; bake for another 5 minutes or until the colour turns light brown.

Deep-fried Fish Paper-wrapped

CHIH BO YU

Preparation and cooking time : 40 minutes

225g (8oz) white fish fillet
   (sliced into 12 pieces)
1 teaspoon salt
1 tablespoon Chinese wine or
   dry sherry
a pinch of pepper
12 slices of ginger

12 snow peas
12 small pieces of sliced leek
12 slices of dried mushroom
2 tablespoons sesame oil or lard
oil for deep-frying
12 greaseproof paper squares,
   10cm (4in)

1. Sprinkle the fish with salt, wine and pepper.
2. Wipe the centre of the greaseproof paper squares with sesame oil or lard and put in one piece each of fish, ginger, peas, leek and mushroom.
3. Fold the paper squares like an envelope and tuck in flap to secure.
4. Heat oil for deep-frying to 180C/350F. Place greaseproof paper packets into oil, flap side up. Deep-fry for 3 minutes until slightly browned.
5. Remove from oil and drain. Serve hot.

Note : To eat, the paper wrapping should be broken in the centre with chopsticks or fork and the paper discarded before eating.

The wrapper will hold in the flavour.

Over-frying the envelopes will cause the meat to stick to the paper. The envelopes retain heat and so the contents will still continue to cook after the envelopes have been removed from the oil.

Deep-fried Fish with Corn

CHA YU

Preparation time : 7 minutes   Cooking time : 10 minutes

450g (1lb) sole or canned tuna
  fish
1 cup whole corn kernels
1 cup flour

½ cup water
oil for deep-frying
a dash of salt
a dash of black pepper

1. Cut the fish into bite-sized pieces. Sprinkle with salt and black pepper.
2. Mix the corn, flour and water into a batter.
3. Heat the oil, dip the fish pieces into the batter and fry them until golden brown. Serve with tomato ketchup or soy sauce as a dip.

Deep-fried Whole Fish

CHA CHUAN YU

Preparation time : 1 hour   Cooking time : 10–20 minutes

1 whole fish (carp, cod, yellow
  pike, bass, butterfish)
1 tablespoon Chinese wine or
  dry sherry
3 tablespoons soy sauce
4 tablespoons cornflour
oil for deep-frying

Sauce
3 tablespoons oil
½ carrot (½ cup after shredding)

1 green pepper (½ cup after
  removing seeds and shredding)
½ bamboo shoot (½ cup after
  shredding)
1 tablespoon tomato sauce
1 tablespoon soy sauce
5 tablespoons sugar
3 tablespoons vinegar
a pinch of salt
1⅓ tablespoons cornflour
1 cup water

1. Fish: scale the whole fish and clean it. Make 3 or 4 parallel diagonal slashes towards the head on each side of the fish. Cut

down deeply and separate the flesh from the bone, however one part should still adhere to the bone.

2. The flesh should separate when the tail is held.

3. Cover the fish with 1 tablespoon wine, 3 tablespoons soy sauce and then coat with 4 tablespoons cornflour. Also rub this into the stomach.

4. Heat a large quantity of oil to 180C/360F. When hot hold the tail of the fish, and taking great care not to touch the boiling fat with your hands, slip it gently into the oil and deep-fry until the colour changes to golden brown (about 10 to 20 minutes depending on the size of the fish).

5. The oil should be enough to cover the fish, if it does not completely do so, keep spooning oil over it with a ladle. Keep pan cover on to prevent oil splattering.

6. Hold spatula in one hand with chopstick or fork in the other. Lift up the fish and drain on a paper towel; place on a plate. Press back with paper towel starting from head and working down to the tail; the fish will stand on its side.

7. Sauce: heat 3 tablespoons oil, the vinegar, sugar, salt, soy sauce and tomato sauce in a pan, stir in green pepper, bamboo shoot and carrot for a short time.

8. Blend the cornflour with the water, add to the mixture in the pan and bring to the boil, stirring constantly until thick.

9. Pour sauce over fish and serve at once.

Note : If you wish to deep-fry fish in advance, fry again to heat through just before serving or heat in oven. This not only saves time but makes the fish crisper.

Fish can be deep-fried either whole or in steaks, strips or rolls.

The Chinese custom to serve the fish whole for special occasions is considered complete and aesthetic.

It is much easier to handle if the fish is cut in pieces.

Freshwater fish can be kept alive in ponds or tubs until ready to be used. Chinese cooking best suits the freshwater varieties.

Flaky Fish

YU SUNG

Preparation time : 20 minutes   *Cooking time : 25 minutes*

450g (1lb) white fish meat
3 slices ginger
12½cm (5in) leek
2 tablespoons Chinese wine or
  dry sherry

1½ teaspoons salt
1 tablespoon soy sauce
1 tablespoon sugar
2 tablespoons oil

1. Cut the fish meat into slices; marinate with the ginger, leek and wine for 20 minutes.
2. Steam for 10 minutes.
3. Heat a pan, add the steamed fish with the liquid and mash finely over a low heat until dry.
4. Add the salt, soy sauce, sugar and oil; continue to stir-fry until the fish becomes flaky and golden brown. Serve with rice or bread.

Note : Flaky Fish will keep for a month in an air-tight jar.

Fried Sliced Fish with Tomato Sauce

FAN CHIEH YU PIEN

Preparation and cooking time : 20 minutes

450g (1lb) white fish, skinned
  and boned
2 tablespoons salad oil
110g (4oz) snow peas
oil for deep-frying
½ tablespoon cornflour
1 cup water

(A)
½ teaspoon ginger juice

1 tablespoon Chinese wine or
  dry sherry
4 tablespoons cornflour

(B)
4 tablespoons tomato ketchup
1 tablespoon Chinese wine or
  dry sherry
1 tablespoon sugar
½ tablespoon salt

1. Slice the fish on bias and soak in ingredients (*A*).
2. String the snow peas.
3. Combine ingredients (*B*). Mix the cornflour with the water.
4. Heat the oil and deep-fry the fish; put into the oil and take out quickly before colouring. Remove to a plate.
5. Heat 2 tablespoons oil and stir-fry the peas a few times. Add (*B*) seasonings. When it boils, add the cornflour mixture and the fish. Stir-fry for 1 minute. Serve hot.

Grilled Fish

KAO YU

Preparation time : 20 minutes   Cooking time : 15 minutes

1 kg (2¼lb) fish	*3 tablespoons soy sauce*
1 teaspoon ginger	*3 tablespoons Chinese wine or*
a pinch of salt	*dry sherry*
1 clove of garlic	

1. Clean and scale the fish; sprinkle with salt.
2. Grate the garlic and ginger, mix with the soy sauce and wine; soak the fish in this for 15 minutes.
3. Bake the fish in a moderate oven or on a charcoal wire grill for 15 minutes.

Smoked Fish

HSUN YU

Preparation time : 3 hours   Cooking time : 1 hour

450g (1lb) fish, sliced
oil for deep-frying

Marinade
4 tablespoons Chinese wine or
   dry sherry
½ cup soy sauce
5 slices ginger
2 tablespoons chopped onion
1 clove garlic, crushed
a pinch of pepper

2 cloves of aniseed
1 teaspoon black peppercorns
   (optional)

Sauce
2 tablespoons Chinese wine or
   dry sherry
2 tablespoons soy sauce
2 tablespoons sesame oil
3 tablespoons brown sugar

1. Soak the fish in the marinade for at least 3 hours or overnight. Heat oil and deep-fry the fish piece by piece until
golden brown.
2. Put all the ingredients for the sauce together in a small pan
and heat until they come to the boil. Dip the fried fish slices
into the sauce and serve hot or cold.

*Note : The fish may be smoked by cooking over brown sugar in a
deep pan. A smoke oven may also be used for this purpose. The
smoking step is optional but gives a delicious taste. Smoked fish
will keep for 4 days, and tastes better every day. It is simple and
easy to prepare.*

Steamed Whole Fish

CHING CHENG CHUAN YU

Preparation time : 15 minutes   Cooking time : 15–20 minutes

1 fish (about ¾kg/1½lb)

(A)
2 dried mushrooms
3 slices bamboo shoots
1 slice ham
85g (3oz) pork suet
1 leek, scallion or onion
3 slices ginger
1 tablespoon Chinese wine or
  dry sherry

½ teaspoon salt
3 tablespoons broth

(B)
1 tablespoon Chinese wine or
  dry sherry
1 tablespoon soy sauce
1 tablespoon vinegar
1 teaspoon sugar
1 teaspoon ginger juice

1. Clean and scale fish. Make 3 slashes on each side of fish.
2. Soak the mushrooms, take off the stems and cut into bite-sized pieces. Cut the ham, bamboo shoots, pork suet, and leek into same size as the mushrooms.
3. Mix ingredients (B) to serve with steamed fish for dipping.
4. Place the fish on a plate, sprinkle all the ingredients (A) on top. Put in a steamer and steam for 15–20 minutes.

Note : If the fish is too long for the steamer, cut into half, then connect it on the plate when serving. Fish slices can be used.

Stuffed Carrot Roll with Minced Fish

HU LU PU JUEN

Preparation time : 20 minutes   Cooking time : 15 minutes

60g (2oz) chopped fish fillet
12 lengthwise slices of carrot
1 large dried mushroom or green
    pepper
2 teaspoons Chinese wine or
    dry sherry
pinch of salt
1 tablespoon chopped parlsey
1 tablespoon cornflour

Sauce
1 teaspoon soy sauce
1 tablespoon wine or sherry
¼ teaspoon salt
¼ teaspoon sugar
2 teaspoons cornflour
½ cup water

1. Cut the carrot slices into 5–7½cm (2–3in) rectangles. Boil in salted water until soft. Soak in cold water; put on a board and make slits along one side of each slice with a knife.
2. Soak the dried mushroom in lukewarm water for 20 minutes. Slice thin, long strips using the black part only, or strip the green pepper.
3. Mix the chopped fish fillet with salt, wine, and cornflour to make the filling.
4. Place about ½ teaspoon of filling on each carrot slice and roll. Garnish with mushroom or green pepper as a band. Press some parsley into the unslit end of rolls.
5. Place on a plate and steam for 10 minutes. Stir all the sauce ingredients over the heat to thicken and pour on top, or serve the carrot rolls with mustard or soy sauce.

Fish Balls

YU WON

Preparation time : 30 minutes   Cooking time : 15 minutes

450g (1lb) fish meat
½ onion or leek chopped
340g (12oz) potato
2 eggs
¾ teaspoon salt
1 tablespoon oil

1 tablespoon Chinese wine or
   dry sherry
2 tablespoons green peas
¼ cup water chestnuts chopped
oil for deep-frying

1. Remove the skin and bone from the fish, boil in water with onion or leek for 10 minutes; drain and break up the meat.
2. Boil the potatoes and mash when cooked.
3. Combine the fish meat, mashed potato, eggs, oil, wine, salt, green peas, and water chestnuts well together.
4. With a tablespoon, form the mixture into balls.
5. Heat the oil and deep-fry until golden brown.

Deep-fried Fish Rolls

CHA YU JUEN

Preparation time : 20 minutes   Cooking time : 20 minutes
(Makes about 14 rolls)

450g (1lb) fish fillet
1 teaspoon ginger juice
a pinch of salt
a dash of pepper
110g (4oz) ham
60g (2oz) bamboo shoot
   (optional)
oil for deep-frying

Batter
2–3 egg whites
3 tablespoons flour
½ teaspoon baking powder

1. Cut the fish fillet into 3½cm by 8cm (2½in by 3½in) slices; sprinkle with ginger juice, salt and pepper.
2. Shred the ham and bamboo shoots into strips.

3. Place 4 to 5 strips of ham with a few strips of bamboo shoots and roll with $\frac{1}{14}$ of the fish.

4. Beat the egg whites until stiff; add the flour and baking powder. Dip the fish rolls in the batter.

5. Heat the oil and add the fish rolls, a few at a time, and deep-fry lightly. Serve with tomato ketchup or a pepper and salt mixture.

Steamed Fish Roll

CHENG YU JUEN

Preparation time : 20 minutes   Cooking time : 20 minutes

450g (1lb) fish fillet
½ teaspoon salt
a dash of pepper
12–14 shrimps
2 tablespoons flour
4 tablespoons water

1 cup broth
2 tablespoons soy sauce
1 tablespoon Chinese wine or
    dry sherry
1 tablespoon cornflour

1. Slice the fish fillet thinly; sprinkle with salt and pepper.

2. Shell the shrimps, remove the black veins, and sprinkle with salt and pepper.

3. Roll the fish fillet pieces with the shrimps. Seal with a flour paste made by mixing the flour with 4 tablespoons water. Place on a plate and steam for 15 minutes.

4. Boil the broth with the soy sauce, wine, and cornflour. Pour on top of the steamed fish and serve.

Lobster Cantonese Style

LUNG HSIA

Preparation time : 15 minutes   *Cooking time : 5 minutes*

1 lobster (about 1kg/2¼lb)
2 cloves garlic
1 teaspoon ginger
4 tablespoons oil
1 tablespoon soy sauce

2 tablespoons Chinese wine or
  dry sherry
1 tablespoon fermented black
  beans
½ cup water or stock

1. Clean the lobster, cut in half lengthwise, and then cut each half into 5cm (2in) sections. Halve the claws.
2. Chop the garlic and ginger and mash the fermented black beans with a little water.
3. Heat the oil; stir-fry the garlic and ginger. When fragrant, add the black beans and lobster and stir-fry quickly; add the wine, soy sauce and water or stock. Cover and simmer for about 3 minutes. Serve hot as soon as the shell turns red and the meat white.

Deep-fried Oyster Balls

LI HUANG JUEN

Preparation time : 15 minutes   *Cooking time : 15 minutes*

20 oysters
1 leek
10 slices bacon
1 teaspoon cornflour
20 cocktail sticks

1 egg
5 tablespoons flour
oil for deep-frying
salt

1. Put the oysters in a drainer, sprinkle with a teaspoon of salt and run water over the top while shaking the drainer so that all the black dust comes out. Drain and parboil for two minutes.
2. Cut the bacon slices into halves. Cut the leek into pieces the same length as the oysters.

3. Roll one oyster and one piece of leek with a piece of bacon and secure with a cocktail stick. Roll in the cornflour.
4. Beat the egg, add a pinch of salt and the flour with sufficient water to make a batter.
5. Dip each oyster in the batter and deep-fry.

Fried Oyster Balls

CHA LI HUANG

Preparation time : 10 minutes   Cooking time : 10 minutes

2 cups chopped oysters
2 tablespoons chopped leek or
    onion
4 eggs
4 tablespoons flour

1 teaspoon baking powder
½ teaspoon salt
a dash of pepper
oil for deep-frying

1. Place the oysters in a strainer. Sprinkle with salt, and wash thoroughly under running water, shaking constantly for about 1 minute.
2. Mix the chopped oysters and leek with all the ingredients. Form into tablespoon-sized balls.
3. Heat the oil to 180C/350F and deep-fry the balls until golden brown.

Sauté Oysters

CHAO LI HUANG

Preparation time : 20 minutes   Cooking time : 5 minutes

340g (12oz) oysters
1½ teaspoons salt
½ teaspoon ginger juice
oil for deep-frying
1 teaspoon soy sauce
½ teaspoon sugar

1 tablespoon Chinese wine or
    dry sherry
a dash of pepper
30g (1oz) transparent vermicelli
2 tablespoons oil
2 cups shredded lettuce

1. Place the oysters in a strainer and sprinkle with salt; wash them under running water, shaking constantly, for about 1 minute.
2. Parboil the oysters and chop. Sprinkle with ginger juice.
3. Cut the transparent vermicelli into about 7½cm (3in) lengths and fry in heated oil until it swells.
4. Place the shredded lettuce and vermicelli on a serving plate.
5. Heat 2 tablespoons oil. Sauté the chopped oysters and add the seasonings, and place on top of the lettuce and vermicelli.

Prawn with Chilli Pepper

KAN SHAO MING HSIA

Preparation time : 15 minutes   Cooking time : 15 minutes

6 king-size prawns	1 egg white
2 leeks	1 tablespoon cornflour
8 chilli peppers	oil for deep-frying
2 slices ginger	1 tablespoon soy sauce
1 teaspoon minced garlic	½ teaspoon salt
1 tablespoon Chinese wine or	2 teaspoons sugar
dry sherry	1 teaspoon vinegar

1. Shell the prawns and remove tails; slit backs and de-vein. Slit each prawn a few times to prevent shrinking, then divide into 3 pieces crosswise.
2. Cut the leeks into 5cm (2in) lengths. Halve the chilli peppers and remove seeds.
3. Combine the soy sauce, sugar, salt, and vinegar in a bowl.
4. Combine the prawn with the wine, egg white and cornflour.
5. Heat plenty of oil; deep-fry the prawns a few at a time and remove to a plate.
6. Heat 3 tablespoons oil and stir-fry the ginger, garlic, leek, and chilli pepper; when fragrant, return the fried prawns to the pan, pour in the seasoning mixture, and bring to the boil.

Deep-fried Salmon Balls

CHA YU CHIU

Preparation time : 10 minutes   Cooking time : 7 minutes

1 can salmon
1 cake bean curd (about 1½ cups)
1 small egg
1 small onion
5 tablespoons cornflour
1 teaspoon salt

1 teaspoon soy sauce
1 teaspoon Chinese wine or
    dry sherry
a dash of pepper
½ teaspoon grated garlic
oil for deep-frying

1. Drain the fish from the can.
2. Break the bean curd with the beaten egg.
3. Chop the onion thoroughly.
4. Mix all the ingredients well and measure with a tablespoon one by one into round balls.
5. Heat some oil, and fry until golden brown. Serve hot.

Note : 1 cake bean curd may be substituted by 2 slices of bread soaked in water.

Shrimp Fried in Egg Batter

CHA HSIA JÊN

Preparation and cooking time : 20 minutes

225g (8oz) shrimps
½ teaspoon salt
1 teaspoon cornflour
2 egg whites
2 tablespoons cornflour
¼ teaspoon salt

oil for deep-frying

Condiments
salt
crushed black peppercorns
tomato sauce

1. Shell and de-vein the shrimps leaving the tails on.
2. On the underside of the shrimps make 5–6 cuts across the muscle to prevent the shrimps from curling up.
3. Sprinkle salt over the shrimps and a teaspoon of cornflour and let them stand for 10 minutes.

4. Beat the egg whites until stiff. Add ¼ teaspoon salt and fold in the 2 tablespoons of cornflour to form a batter.
5. Heat the oil for deep-frying to 160C/320F. Dip the shrimps in the batter and deep-fry about 6 at a time for about 2 minutes. Remove quickly and drain on paper. The shrimps should not become dark coloured – do not overcook. Serve immediately with condiments.

Note : Black peppercorns taste very good as a condiment with the shrimps. Heat 1 tablespoon of black peppercorns with 1 table-spoon salt in a dry pan over low heat. Shake and stir until the salt turns slightly brown and the peppercorns become fragrant. Re-move from the pan and let cool. Crush the peppercorns with a rolling pin, then strain through a sieve. Two teaspoons ground black pepper may be substituted for the peppercorns.

Stir-fried Shrimp with Broccoli

HSIA JÊN CHAO GAI LAN

Preparation time : 10 minutes Cooking time : 3 minutes

450g (1lb) shrimps
½ teaspoon ginger juice or minced
   ginger
2 teaspoons cornflour
1 head broccoli*
5 tablespoons oil

1 teaspoon salt
2 tablespoons Chinese wine or
   dry sherry
1–2 tablespoons water
1 teaspoon sugar

1. Shell and de-vein the shrimps; remove the tails. Combine with the ginger juice and cornflour; let stand for 5 minutes.
2. Separate the broccoli into flowerets and boil in salted water until tender. Trim off the tough ends and cut the stems diagonally into 1cm (½in) lengths.
3. Heat the oil and stir-fry the shrimps over a high heat until their colour changes; add the broccoli stems, then stir in the flowerets, salt, sugar, wine, and water. Boil for 1 minute, and serve hot.

* *Green asparagus can be substituted for broccoli.*

Eggs

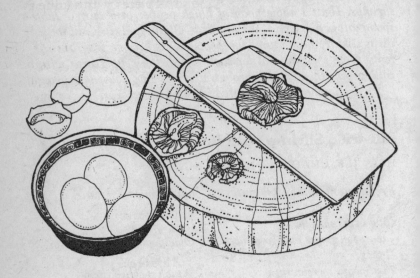

Baked Egg

KAO TAN

Preparation time : 10 minutes   Cooking time : 20 minutes

6 eggs
1 teaspoon salt
110g (4oz) minced chicken
½ cup shredded bamboo shoots
½ cup shredded dried mushrooms
2 tablespoons salad oil

Seasonings
1 tablespoon soy sauce
2 teaspoons sugar
1 tablespoon Chinese wine or
    dry sherry
¼ cup broth or water

1. Break the eggs into a bowl; add salt and beat.
2. Soak the mushrooms in water, take off the stems and shred.
3. Heat the oil and fry the chicken meat until it changes colour. Then add the bamboo shoots, mushrooms, and the seasonings. Remove from heat and mix in the beaten eggs after mixture has cooled.
4. Pour the mixture into a greased baking pan and bake in a moderate oven (180C/350F/Mark 4) for 20 minutes.
5. Remove to a plate and cut into small pieces with a knife at the table.

Note : Test with a fork or skewer to tell if the egg mixture is done. When cooked, it will not stick to the skewer. Dried mushrooms can be substituted with fresh mushrooms.

Crab Fu Yung

FU JUNG HSIEH

Preparation time : 10 minutes   Cooking time : 10 minutes

1 cup crab meat, fresh or canned
1 tablespoon Chinese wine or
    dry sherry
4 egg whites
¾ teaspoon salt

2 tablespoons cornflour
7 tablespoons oil
1 cup milk
1 tablespoon chopped parsley
1.tablespoon chopped ham

1. Remove fragments of shell from the crab meat.
2. Mix the crab meat with wine.
3. Beat the egg whites until stiff; add salt and cornflour.
4. Heat the oil and let it spread over the frying-pan.
5. Mix the crab meat and milk with the egg white.
6. Pour the mixture into the frying-pan. Stir constantly until it thickens.
7. Remove to a plate and sprinkle with chopped parsley and chopped ham. Serve hot.

Note : If fresh crab is used, steam first for 30 minutes and take out the meat from the shell.

Eggs Boiled with Tea Leaves

CHA YEH TAN

Preparation and cooking time : 40 minutes

8 eggs
2 tablespoons black or Jasmine
   tea
1 tablespoon peppercorns
   (optional)

3 cloves aniseed (optional)
parsley for decoration
¾ tablespoon salt
4 tablespoons soy sauce

1. Put the well-washed eggs slowly into a large pan of warm water. Carefully move the eggs around while bringing the water to the boil – 2–3 minutes – to make the egg yolks stay in the centre.
2. From the time the water begins to boil, cook the eggs for 7 minutes; cool in cold water.
3. Lightly tap the surface of the egg shell with a spoon until it is cracked all over.
4. Return the eggs to the pan, add the black tea, aniseed, peppercorns, soy sauce and salt and cover with water. Bring to the boil.
5. Turn the flame down so that the water simmers for 20 minutes, or until the egg shell has turned brown. Turn off the heat. Cool the eggs in the liquid. Drain. Remove the shells.
6. Cut the eggs in half lengthwise, or serve whole. Be careful not to break the yolk. Serve the eggs on a plate with the cut surface up. Decorate with parsley.

Note : Eggs should be at room temperature before placing in hot water ; eggs just from the refrigerator will crack easily. Cracking the egg shell all over will allow the tea liquid to seep through and flavour the eggs. It gives the eggs a marble look, like antique porcelain. They are excellent for picnics. If you want to keep them for a few days before eating, leave the eggs in their shells as this will keep them moist.

Fried Egg with Chopped Leek

ZIAG CHI TANG

Preparation and cooking time : 7 minutes

4 eggs	½ teaspoon salt
2 tablespoons chopped leek or onion	4 tablespoons oil

1. Beat the eggs in a bowl; add the salt and chopped leek or onion and mix well.
2. Heat the oil and when it is very hot, pour the egg mixture into a pan and spread around evenly. Cook until golden brown on both sides.
3. Serve either whole or cut into pieces.

Fried Egg with Fish Meat

KUEI HUA YU SUNG

Preparation time : 20 minutes   Cooking time : 5 minutes

225g (8oz) white fish meat	1 tablespoon Chinese wine or
4 eggs	dry sherry
4 tablespoons salad oil	⅓ teaspoon salt

(A)	(B)
2 onions, cut into 5cm (2in) lengths	1 teaspoon salt
3 slices ginger	½ teaspoon sugar

1. Marinate the fish with ingredients (A) for 5 minutes. Steam for 10 minutes. Divide the meat into pieces.
2. Beat the eggs and add ingredients (B) and the fish.
3. Heat the oil in a pan. Fry the egg mixture until it sets. Serve hot.

Stir-fried Egg with Dried Shrimps

HAI MI CHAO TAN

Preparation and cooking time : 10 minutes

6 eggs	4 tablespoons dried shrimps
2 tablespoons Chinese wine or	½ teaspoon salt
dry sherry	5 tablespoons oil

1. Place the shrimps in a small bowl and wash thoroughly to remove sand. Cover with lukewarm water and soak for 10 minutes until softened. Drain. Sprinkle with 1 tablespoon of wine.
2. Break the eggs into a bowl, beat well with chopsticks or a fork. Add the salt, shrimps and all the wine and mix well.
3. Heat the oil in a pan over a strong heat. Turn the pan to spread the oil over as much of its surface as possible. As soon as the oil is lightly smoking quickly pour in the egg mixture.
4. Turn down the heat to medium and scramble the eggs until they are set – tender but no longer glossy. Transfer to a warm plate and serve at once.

Note : Be careful not to overcook the eggs as they will continue to cook in the pan after it has been removed from the heat.

Scrambled Egg with Tomato

FAN CHIEH CHAO TAN

Preparation and cooking time : 5 minutes

4 eggs	½ teaspoon salt
1 tomato	5 tablespoons oil

1. Dip the tomato into boiling water, remove the skin and cut into cubes, removing the seeds.
2. Beat the eggs and add the salt.
3. Heat a pan and add the oil. Fry the egg mixture until partly set, then add the tomato and mix for 2 minutes.

Steamed Eggs

CHENG TAN

Preparation and cooking time : 25 minutes

3 eggs	½ cup canned sweet corn, whole
1 cup stock	grain
1 teaspoon salt	½ teaspoon ginger juice
110g (4oz) wood ear or dried	½ teaspoon cornflour
mushrooms	2 teaspoons soy sauce
110g (4oz) small shrimps	2 tablespoons oil

1. Beat the eggs very well. Add the stock and ½ teaspoon salt and mix well. Pour the egg mixture into a deep serving dish that will fit into a steamer. Remove any bubbles from the top.
2. Place a Chinese wok (pan) on the stove and fill with water up to 2½cm (1in) below the bamboo rack. Bring the water in the pan to a rapid boil. Place the serving dish containing the egg mixture on the bamboo rack over the boiling water. Cover with the bamboo steamer lid. Reduce the heat to medium, and steam for 15 minutes. To test that the custard is set, prick the centre with a cocktail stick. If it is not done continue steaming and test every 2 minutes until cooked. While the custard is steaming, prepare the other ingredients.
3. Shell and de-vein the shrimps. Marinate in the ginger juice and cornflour.
4. Soak the dried mushrooms in lukewarm water to make them tender. Drain and slice.
5. Drain the sweet corn.
6. When custard is done heat the pan, add 2 tablespoons oil and heat again. Add the shrimps and stir-fry for about 1 minute; as soon as colour changes, add the mushrooms and sweet corn and cook for about 1 minute. Then add the soy sauce and salt and quickly stir until well blended and all the ingredients are very hot. This should take no more than 2½ to 3 minutes. Carefully pour the mixture on top of the steamed custard. Serve hot.

Note : The serving dish in Step 1 should be large enough to hold about 4 cups of liquid. In Step 2 the egg and stock mixture may separate if it is left standing too long. It should be steamed immediately after being prepared.

If a metal steamer is used, be sure to place a cloth (cheese cloth or a tea towel) between the lid and the bowl to catch the moisture which collects on the underside of the cover. Bring the edges of the cloth up over the top of the cover and tie to prevent the cloth catching on fire. If the moisture drops onto the surface of the egg mixture, it will form holes in the custard.

Be careful not to oversteam.

Steamed Egg Custard with Chicken

CHENG TAN KUNG

Preparation time : 10 minutes   Cooking time : 15 minutes

4 eggs	*2 tablespoons mushroom, cubed*
3 cups broth or water	*1 teaspoon sesame oil*
1½ teaspoons salt	*2 teaspoons soy sauce*
¼ cup chicken meat, cubed	

1. Beat the eggs and blend with the broth or water; add the salt, chicken meat and mushroom.
2. Place in a bowl and steam for 15 minutes.
3. Sprinkle with the sesame oil and soy sauce when serving.

Vegetables and Salads

Sauté Asparagus with Scallop

CHAO SHIAN PEI

Preparation time : 12 minutes   Cooking time : 6 minutes

450g (1lb) asparagus
110g (4oz) ham
225g (8oz) scallops
1 teaspoon ginger juice
3 tablespoons salad oil
½ cup chicken broth

1 teaspoon salt
1 teaspoon sugar
1 tablespoon Chinese wine or
  dry sherry
2 teaspoons cornflour
2 teaspoons water

1. Wash the asparagus and cut off the tough parts of the stem; boil in salted water for about 15 minutes or until tender, using a coffee pot or a similar container to prevent hurting the tips.
2. Drain. Peel the hard skin off. Cut each length into 2 or 3 pieces.
3. Slice the ham; divide each slice into 4 pieces. Wash the scallops in salt water, remove the hard piece in the centre and remove the thin skin; slice into 6 pieces, mix with 1 teaspoon ginger juice and 1 teaspoon cornflour. Parboil in water briefly; drain.
4. Heat the oil and fry the asparagus until the oil starts to soak in. Add the scallop, ham, broth and seasonings. When it boils, add 1 teaspoon cornflour mixed with 2 teaspoons water, stirring constantly. Serve hot.

Note : Instead of boiling asparagus whole, it may be cut up first ; boil the lower stalks for 5 minutes longer than the tips.

Braised Aubergine with Chilli Pepper

GAN SAO CHIE ZU

Preparation time : 10 minutes   Cooking time : 10 minutes

450g (1lb) aubergine*
225g (8oz) green pepper
1 hot red chilli pepper
4 tablespoons oil

1 teaspoon sugar
1 tablespoon soy bean paste or
 2 tablespoons soy sauce

1. Wash the aubergine, discard the stem, shred and soak in water for 5 minutes. Drain.
2. Halve the green peppers; remove the seeds and shred.
3. Halve the chilli pepper; remove the seeds and shred.
4. Heat the oil in a pan; stir-fry the aubergine, green pepper, chilli pepper and add the seasonings. Turn the flame low; simmer until the juice disappears.

* *If the skin of the aubergine is tough it should be peeled.*

Deep-fried Bean Curd Balls

CHA TOU FU WON TZU

Preparation time : 20 minutes   Cooking time : 10 minutes

3 cups bean curd   1 teaspoon salt
1 cup shrimps   1 egg
1 cup spinach   4 tablespoons cornflour
1 tablespoon Chinese wine or   oil for deep-frying
  dry sherry

1. Break up the bean curd; shell the shrimps, remove the black veins and chop coarsely.
2. Wash the spinach; parboil and chop coarsely.
3. Mix all the ingredients together, except the oil. Form into balls.
4. Heat some oil and deep-fry the bean curd balls. Serve with the following three sauces.

Note : If frozen spinach is used, defrost and squeeze out the water.

(I) SWEET AND SOUR SAUCE

2 tablespoons sugar   1 tablespoon cornflour
1 tablespoon soy sauce   ½ cup water
1 tablespoon vinegar

Mix all the ingredients; heat in a pot and stir until thickened. Serve in a small container.

(II) SOY BEAN PASTE SAUCE

Made from soy beans and can be bought ready-made in a can or bag.

(III) SESAME PASTE SAUCE

Mix with salt. Sesame paste sauce can be bought ready-made. Peanut butter may be substituted.

Note : Since bean curd is a soya bean product, and therefore a natural food, use as often as possible.

Bean Curd with Chilli Sauce

MA PO TOU FU

Preparation time : 20 minutes   Cooking time : 15 minutes

2 cakes bean curd (¾kg/1½lb)
110g (4oz) minced pork or beef
4 tablespoons oil
2 tablespoons chopped leek
1 tablespoon grated garlic
1 chilli pepper (or 1 teaspoon chilli powder)
1 tablespoon Chinese wine or dry sherry

2 tablespoons soy sauce
1 tablespoon soy bean paste
1 tablespoon black fermented bean (optional)
¾ cup broth or water
½ teaspoon hot chilli oil (optional)
2 tablespoons cornflour
2 tablespoons water

1. Boil the bean curd in plenty of lightly salted water. Remove it from the water and place it on a cheese cloth to drain.
2. After the bean curd has drained, cut it into small 1cm (½in) cubes.
3. Halve the red chilli pepper, remove the seeds and chop it; also chop the leek.
4. Melt the bean paste with 2 tablespoons soy sauce; set aside. Mix 1 tablespoon cornflour with 1 tablespoon water.
5. Heat a pan, add 4 tablespoons oil and stir-fry the leek and garlic over a strong heat until garlic becomes fragrant; add the chilli pepper, black fermented bean and then the meat and stir until the meat changes colour, add the wine, bean paste, and the broth or water, boil for 10 minutes and thicken with the cornflour mixture.

6. Sprinkle with chopped leek and hot chilli oil; mix and serve hot.

Note : Once the bean curd has boiled, it will not be so easy to break up ; also it will not get too watery.

This dish will easily burn after the minced meat has been added. Therefore, quick stirring is necessary. Keep it from sticking by gently shaking the pan.

Chopped chilli pepper cooked in hot oil and then drained can be used as hot chilli oil.

Black fermented bean is preserved soy beans. It is salty and black in colour.

Steamed Bean Curd with Salted Fish

CHENG HSING YU TOU FU

Preparation time : 15 minutes   Cooking time : 15 minutes

2 cakes bean curd
salt
pepper
225g (8oz) salted fish
½ stalk of leek (½ cup after
  chopping)

60g (2oz) dried shrimp
1 tablespoon Chinese wine or
  dry sherry
2 tablespoons soy sauce
2 teaspoons sesame oil

1. Break the bean curd in a bowl and sprinkle with salt and pepper.
2. Cube the fish and soak the dried shrimp in warm water.
3. Chop the leek.
4. Add the cubed fish, soaked dried shrimp, chopped leek and wine to the bean curd; steam for 15 minutes.
5. Add the soy sauce and sesame oil gradually, checking the taste, as salted fish and dried shrimp can be very salty.
6. Serve with a spoon.

Braised Broccoli

HUI GAI LAN

Preparation and cooking time : 25 minutes

225g (8oz) broccoli	½ teaspoon salt
3 tablespoons chopped ham	1½ cups broth
2 tablespoons oil	1 tablespoon cornflour
¼ teaspoon sugar	1 tablespoon water

1. Wash the broccoli in cold water with a little salt. Cut the flowerets off into pieces about 4–5cm (1½–2in) long. Peel the outside of the fibrous stalk and slice it into pieces about 5cm (2in) long and less than 1cm (½in) thick.
2. Parboil the stalk for about 4 to 6 minutes, and then drop the flowerets into the boiling water for a second or two. Drain.
3. Heat the oil in a pan; stir-fry the broccoli. Add the sugar, salt and broth and boil until tender. Thicken with a cornflour and water mixture. Pour into a serving dish. Sprinkle with chopped ham.

Braised Chinese Cabbage with Crab Meat

HSIEH JOU PAI TSAI

Preparation time : 15 minutes   Cooking time : 5 minutes

450g (1lb) Chinese cabbage	1–1½ teaspoons salt
225g (8oz) can crab meat	½ teaspoon sugar
2 tablespoons salad oil	pepper
1 tablespoon Chinese wine or	1 tablespoon cornflour
dry sherry	2 tablespoons water

1. Remove the outside leaves of the Chinese cabbage; use the white lower parts. Slice the leaves and shred.
2. Parboil in salted water; drain.
3. Remove any bones from the crab meat and break into fragments.

4. Stir-fry the cabbage in heated oil. Add the crab meat and stir-fry for 1 minute. Add the seasonings and the cornflour mixed with water; braise until it becomes starchy. Serve hot.

Note : Green parts of the cabbage may also be used, or kept for soups.

Cabbage Salad with Sesame Seeds

YANG PAI TSAI PAN CHIH MA

Preparation time : 15 minutes   Cooking time : 10 minutes

*450g (1lb) cabbage (about half a   1 teaspoon dry mustard
  head)   1 tablespoon soy sauce
½ teaspoon salt   2 tablespoons vinegar
4 tablespoons sesame seeds or   2 slices ham
  2 tablespoons sesame oil*

1. Discard the outside leaves of the cabbage and remove the hard core. Cut into bite-sized pieces.
2. Wash the cabbage and sprinkle with ½ teaspoon salt. Let stand for 10 minutes.
3. Heat a frying-pan; toast the sesame seeds, shaking the pan all the time.
4. Remove the sesame seeds from the pan when they puff up; crush with a rolling pin.
5. Squeeze the water out of the cabbage, arrange on a platter and put the shredded ham on top.
6. Mix the mustard with the same amount of water; add all the other seasonings, including the crushed sesame seeds.
7. Pour the sauce over the salad before serving. Serve cold.

Sauté Chinese Cabbage

CHAO YANG PAI TSAI

Preparation time : 15 minutes   Cooking time : 10 minutes

450g (1lb) Chinese cabbage	*1 teaspoon sugar*
2 tablespoons oil	*½ teaspoon salt*
2 tablespoons vinegar	*1 teaspoon hot chilli sauce*
1 tablespoon soy sauce	*(Tabasco)*

1. Separate the leaves of the Chinese cabbage; wash and cut into bite-sized pieces.
2. Mix all the seasonings in a bowl.
3. Heat the oil. Sauté the Chinese cabbage over a strong flame.
4. Add the sauce from the bowl, stir and serve either hot or cold.

Sauté Chinese Cabbage with Clams

CHAO PAI TSAI KO LI

Preparation time : 25 minutes   Cooking time : 5 minutes

¾kg (about 1½lb) Chinese	*½ teaspoon salt*
* cabbage**	*¼ teaspoon sugar*
225g (8oz) clams	*2 teaspoons soy sauce*
1 clove garlic	*1 tablespoon Chinese wine or*
2 tablespoons oil	* dry sherry*

1. Separate the Chinese cabbage leaves; cut into bite-sized pieces, parboil for 3 minutes and drain.
2. Parboil the clams for 3 minutes.
3. Heat the oil in a pan. Stir-fry the Chinese cabbage and clams. Add the seasonings and serve hot.

* If you are unable to obtain Chinese cabbage it may be substituted with green leafy cabbage.

Steamed Cabbage Rolls

CHENG YANG PAI TSAI JUEN

Preparation and cooking time : 50 minutes

6 pieces Chinese cabbage (inner part)
cornflour
60g (2oz) ham
225g (8oz) chicken meat
1 teaspoon Chinese wine or dry sherry
½ teaspoon salt

3 dried mushrooms
30g (1oz) vermicelli
1 cup stock
½ teaspoon sugar
2 teaspoons soy sauce
a pinch of salt
1½ teaspoons water

1. Soak the dried mushrooms in lukewarm water for 20 minutes and remove stem. Cut the caps into bite-sized pieces.
2. Soak the vermicelli and cut into 15cm (6in) lengths.
3. Separate the cabbage leaves and boil in water until tender.
4. Drain cabbage and sprinkle with some cornflour on one side.
5. Chop ham finely; mix well with chicken meat, wine, salt and 2 teaspoons cornflour. Divide into 6 portions.
6. Place the meat portions on the lower part of the cabbage leaves. Turn left and right sides over the meat and roll up. Seal with a little more cornflour. If the white part of the cabbage is too thick, it is easier to roll if you separate it like a pocket and then roll.
7. Arrange on a plate and steam for 15 minutes.
8. Cut the cabbage rolls in half and arrange in a pan. Add the mushrooms, vermicelli, stock, sugar, soy sauce, salt and simmer gently for about 5 minutes. Thicken with a mixture of 1½ teaspoons each of cornflour and water. Transfer to a plate.

Sweet and Sour Cabbage

TANG TSU YANNG PAI TSAI

Preparation and cooking time : 15 minutes

450g (1lb) cabbage
1 clove garlic
4 tablespoons salad oil
1 tablespoon vinegar

1 tablespoon soy sauce
2 tablespoons sugar
½ teaspoon salt

1. Remove the outer leaves of the cabbage and divide into 4 pieces.
2. Remove the hard stems. Cut each cabbage quarter into bite-sized pieces. Wash and drain.
3. Crush the garlic with a knife back.
4. Heat the oil and fry the garlic. When it turns light brown, add the cabbage and fry over a strong flame for 3 minutes.
5. Before the cabbage starts to shrivel, add the seasonings, stirring constantly. Serve hot or chilled.

Cucumber and Agar Agar Salad

YANG FEN PAN HUAG KUA

Prepare well in advance   Cooking time : 40 minutes

1 cucumber
a dash of salt
1 agar agar* (15g/½oz)
1 egg
cooking oil
110g (4oz) chicken meat
1 slice ginger
5cm (2in) leek

60g (2oz) ham

Sauce
1 tablespoon sesame oil
1 teaspoon dry mustard
1½ tablespoons soy sauce
1 tablespoon vinegar

1. Beat the egg lightly; add the dash of salt. Heat a pan. Apply a coating of oil to the pan with a brush or paper. Turn the flame down when pan smokes slightly.

2. Pour in ⅓ of the egg mixture, turning the pan around so that the egg spreads into a very thin sheet. It will cook very quickly, but be sure that the egg is done and has lost its glossy look before turning out onto a plate to cool. Repeat the process two more times.

3. Cut each round of egg in half. Stack all the pieces together, roll swiss-roll fashion and with a sharp knife shred into ½cm (¼in) strips. Shake apart.

4. Wash the cucumber in lightly salted water. Slice diagonally, and cut into shreds.

5. Place the chicken, ginger and leek in a pan with just enough water to cover. Bring to the boil, turn the flame down and simmer for 20 minutes or until tender. Strain off the liquid and cool. (The mixture can be cooled more quickly by running tap water over it.) Cut the chicken into slices then shred.

6. Shred the ham.

7. Soak the agar agar in lukewarm water with a dash of salt, changing water 2 or 3 times. Drain well, cut into 5cm (2in) sections.

8. Combine the ingredients for the sauce in a small bowl. Mix well.

9. Arrange the shredded eggs, cucumber, chicken, ham and agar agar in attractive rows on a serving plate. Chill thoroughly in a refrigerator.

10. Just before serving pour the sauce over the salad.

11. Toss at the table.

* *Vermicelli of green bean type may be used instead of the agar agar. Agar agar, or aga-aga, is a dried seaweed, which looks like transparent noodles. It is prepared in long thin strips and can be used as gelatine. Used as gelatine, it must first be soaked in cold lightly salted water, and squeezed to remove as much water as possible. Then when boiling water is poured over it, it will melt. Agar agar can be used for salad and desserts, but the ingredients must be placed in the gelatine while it is still hot, as it should not be stirred once it begins to set.*

Garlic Cucumber

SUAN HUAG KUA

Preparation and cooking time : about 2 hours

2 cucumbers	2 tablespoons sesame oil
½ teaspoon salt	1 tablespoon soy sauce
½ clove garlic	

1. Peel the cucumbers and, if necessary, scoop out the seeds; slice and shred very thinly. Sprinkle with the salt and let stand for 1–2 hours, then drain.
2. Grate the garlic; combine with the sesame oil and soy sauce. Add to the shredded cucumber and toss to mix well. Serve cold.

Sesame Cucumber

CHIH MA HUANG KUA

Preparation time : 1–2 hours   Cooking time : 10 minutes

2 cucumbers	2 tablespoons sesame oil
½ teaspoon salt	¼ teaspoon sugar

1. Peel the cucumbers and cut into half lengthwise. The seeds may be retained or scooped out with a spoon. Cut crosswise in 1cm (½in) slices. Sprinkle with salt and let stand for 1–2 hours. Drain.
2. Heat the sesame oil; add the cucumber and stir-fry for about 30 seconds. Add sugar and stir. Serve cold.

Sweet and Sour Cucumbers

TANG TSU HUANG KUA

Cooking time : 10 minutes

2 cucumbers
1 tablespoon oil
1 small red chilli pepper, seeded
  and shredded

1 tablespoon vinegar
½ teaspoon salt
1 teaspoon sugar

1. Wash the cucumber. Peel if the skin is tough. Cut into 5cm
(2in) lengths and quarter lengthwise; scoop out the seeds.
2. Heat the oil; add the chilli pepper and stir-fry for one
second. Then add the cucumbers and stir-fry for 30 seconds.
Add the seasonings and stir-fry for a further 1 or 2 seconds
until well blended. As soon as the mixture has cooled place in
a refrigerator with the liquid.
3. To serve, remove the cucumbers from the liquid and
sprinkle with a few drops of vinegar.

Stuffed Green Pepper with Fish Fillet

CHING CHIAO CHAI YU MO

Preparation time : 20 minutes   Cooking time : 15 minutes

5 green peppers
225g (8oz) fish fillet
1 teaspoon ginger juice
1 teaspoon Chinese wine or dry
  sherry
1 teaspoon cornflour
a dash of pepper
3 tablespoons oil
1 teaspoon salt

½ teaspoon sugar
½ cup water

Sauce
½ cup water
1 tablespoon soy sauce
½ teaspoon salt
½ teaspoon sugar
2 teaspoons cornflour

1. Halve the green peppers and remove the seeds.

2. Mince the fish fillet; add the ginger juice, wine, $\frac{1}{2}$ teaspoon salt, pepper, and cornflour and mix well.
3. Stuff the green peppers.
4. Heat the oil and cook the open sides of the peppers in the oil until they change colour.
5. Add $\frac{1}{2}$ teaspoon salt, sugar, wine and water to the pan and boil over a medium heat until the water evaporates. Remove to a plate.
6. Boil the sauce, stirring constantly; when thickened pour on the stuffed green peppers.

Lettuce with Milk Sauce

NAI YU TSAI SHIN

Preparation time : 5 minutes   Cooking time : 15 minutes

1 lettuce (about 450g/1lb)	*dash of pepper*
3 tablespoons oil	*$\frac{1}{2}$ teaspoon cornflour*
1$\frac{1}{2}$ teaspoons salt	*1 teaspoon water*
2$\frac{1}{2}$ cups broth	*1 tablespoon chopped ham*
$\frac{1}{2}$ cup milk	*1 tablespoon chopped parsley*

1. Wash the lettuce and cut into 4 portions.
2. Heat the oil; stir-fry the lettuce, add 1 teaspoon salt and the broth and simmer until the lettuce becomes tender. Remove the lettuce from the pan and transfer to a plate; reserve the broth.
3. Boil $\frac{1}{2}$ cup broth, add the milk, salt and pepper. Mix the cornflour and water together and use to thicken the mixture; pour over the lettuce. Sprinkle over the ham and parsley; serve hot.

Braised Dried Mushroom

HUI TUNG KU

Preparation time : 5 minutes   Cooking time : 20 minutes

60g (2oz) dried mushrooms	1 tablespoon sugar
3 tablespoons oil	1 tablespoon sesame oil
2 tablespoons soy sauce	¾ cup water or broth
1 tablespoon Chinese wine or	2 teaspoons cornflour
dry sherry	2 tablespoons water

1. Soak the mushrooms in 2 tablespoons lukewarm water for 20 minutes. Squeeze out the water (saving it for later) and discard the stems.
2. Heat 3 tablespoons oil and stir-fry the mushrooms over a medium heat for a few minutes; add the sugar, sesame oil, soy sauce, and wine. Lower the heat and simmer for 15 minutes with the broth and the mushroom soaking liquid. Add the cornflour; mix to thicken. Serve with bird's nest or separately. Any left over will keep in a refrigerator for the next meal.

Soy Bean Milk

TOU CHIANG

Prepare beans 1 day ahead   Cooking time : 30 minutes

450g (1lb) soy beans	chopped spring onions
9 cups water	dried shrimp
½ cup sugar	hot pepper oil
or	sesame oil
chopped Szechuan pickle	soy sauce

1. Wash the soy beans and soak with enough water to cover overnight.
2. Remove the skins from the beans. Put the beans in an

electric blender and blend at high speed until fine; put in a cheese cloth bag and squeeze out the liquid.

3. Heat 9 cups water and add the squeezed liquid; simmer for 30 minutes. Serve with sugar as sweet soy bean milk or add the pickle, spring onion, shrimp, hot pepper oil, sesame oil and soy sauce and serve as salty bean milk. This is a natural nutrition food.

Pastries and Rice

Deep-fried Bread Stuffed with Shrimp

CHA MEIIN PO HSIA

Preparation time : 20 minutes   *Cooking time : 20 minutes*

110g (4oz) shrimps
110g (4oz) crab meat
2 teaspoons Chinese wine or
* dry sherry*
½ teaspoon salt

a dash of pepper
3 tablespoons cornflour
340g (12oz) sliced bread
oil for deep-frying

1. Shell the shrimps, remove the black veins and chop finely.
2. Remove the bone from the crab meat.

3. Mix the chopped shrimp and crab meat with the wine, salt, pepper, and cornflour.

4. Trim 1cm (½in) crusts off the bread; lay the slices flat and carefully cut slits through the centre to make pockets and stuff with the shrimp mixture.

5. Steam for 10 minutes.

6. Heat the oil in a pan and deep-fry until a golden brown colour.

7. Cut each piece into 3 crosswise. Arrange on a plate in a fan shape.

Chilled Noodles

LENG PAN MEIN

Preparation and cooking time : 40 minutes

225g (8oz) noodles
2 tablespoons sesame oil
1 cucumber, shredded
110g (4oz) bean sprouts (cooked)
1 egg (cooked as egg sheets and
  cut into strips)
a little oil
110g (4oz) chicken (cooked)
½ teaspoon salt
1 tablespoon Chinese wine or
  dry sherry

Sauce
2 tablespoons sesame paste
2 tablespoons soy sauce
2 tablespoons water
hot red chilli oil or Tabasco
  (optional)
¾ cup broth or water
a pinch of salt
a dash of sugar
2 tablespoons vinegar
a dash of pepper

1. Bring some water to the boil with ½ teaspoon salt; add the noodles gradually so that the water remains boiling. Stir and separate the noodles to prevent them sticking together; when the water boils up fiercely again, add one cup of cold water and bring to the boil again. Rinse under cold water and drain. The noodles should be cooked until tender, but remain firm; they should not be mushy.

2. Toss the noodles in sesame oil; allow to cool to room temperature then put in the refrigerator to chill.

3. Place the chilled noodles in a bowl and arrange the meat, egg strips and vegetables on top of the noodles. Mix the sauce ingredients, pour over the meat and vegetables, and toss before serving.

Note : To make sesame paste, toast some sesame seeds in a pan, grind and mix with oil. Sesame paste can be bought in a bottle or substituted with peanut butter.
  Variations : for the chicken, substitute beef, pork, shrimp or ham. One of the vegetables can be omitted.

Fried Noodles

CHAO MIEN

Preparation and cooking time : 25 minutes

There are two kinds of fried noodles :

Soft-fried : lightly browned and crisp on the outside, but still soft inside.

Hard-fried : deep fry until golden brown and crisp.

450g (1lb) noodles – use either egg noodles or wheat flour noodles
110g (4oz) pork or beef sliced
1 teaspoon soy sauce
1 teaspoon cornflour
6 wood ears or mushrooms
1 piece Chinese cabbage or ordinary cabbage
2½cm (1in) leek
2 slices ham

1 teaspoon Chinese wine or dry sherry
1 teaspoon salt
½ teaspoon sugar
3 cups soup stock or water
2 tablespoons cornflour
2 tablespoons water
2 tablespoons oil for stir-frying meat and vegetables
3 tablespoons oil for soft-frying noodles or oil for deep-frying (hard-fried) noodles

1. Parboil the noodles. Rinse off the excess starch and drain. Toss with a little sesame oil to prevent the noodles sticking together.

2. Heat a pan; add the oil for frying the noodles and heat again. Place the noodles in the hot oil and stir with a fork or chopsticks to separate strands. When hot through, reduce the heat and fry one side until golden brown. Turn over, and fry the other side until golden brown. Additional oil may be added from the side of pan.

3. Place the noodles on a plate for serving. Cover with a cheese cloth and press with your hand toward the centre to make the noodles separate. Keep in a warm place. (If the noodles are deep fried, press to crack.)

4. Cut the pork into 2½cm (1in) cubes; add 1 teaspoon soy sauce and 1 teaspoon cornflour for marinade. Set aside.

5. Wash the wood ears or mushrooms and soak in lukewarm water. Remove and discard the hard portion. Cut the cabbage and the ham into bite-sized pieces. Cut the leek into sections.

6. Heat 2 tablespoons oil in a pan until very hot; add the pork and leek and stir-fry for about 1 minute, or until the pork changes colour. Then add the cabbage, wood ear and ham in that order, while continuing to stir-fry.

7. Add the wine, salt, sugar, soup stock or water and boil for 5 minutes.

8. Mix 2 tablespoons cornflour and 2 tablespoons water and add to the mixture in the pan stirring thoroughly. Continue cooking until thickened. Pour on top of the fried noodles. Serve hot.

Sauté Chinese Noodles with Ginger

CHAO MIEN

Preparation time : 15 minutes   *Cooking time : 10 minutes*

450g (1lb) Chinese noodles*
1 cup shredded leek
¼ cup shredded ginger
1 tablespoon Chinese wine or
  dry sherry

2 tablespoons oil
½ cup broth
1 tablespoon soy sauce
a dash of black pepper

1. Bring the noodles to the boil and then add one cup of cold water; repeat the process twice. Drain the noodles, rinse and drain again.

2. Heat the oil in a pan and sauté the leek and ginger; add the noodles, wine, soy sauce, black pepper, and broth; stir for a few minutes and serve.

* *Italian spaghetti or noodles can be substituted.*

Mandarin Pancake Rolls (Peking Pan Cakes)

PO BIEN

Preparation time : 50 minutes   Cooking time : 20 minutes

2 cups plain flour $1\frac{1}{2}$ tablespoons sesame oil
3–4 cups water

1. Boil the water, gradually add it to the flour, while mixing with a wooden spoon or chopstick. Transfer the dough to a board and knead to a soft dough. Cover with a damp towel and let stand for at least 15 minutes.

2. Flour the board lightly. Roll and pull out the dough into a long sausage about 5cm (2in) in diameter.

3. Cut the sausage into 1cm ($\frac{1}{2}$in) pieces. Flatten each piece with your palm, brush the surfaces lightly with sesame oil and stack the pieces in pairs. Dust the outside surface lightly with flour.

4. Roll each pair into a thin pancake with a rolling pin about 10–12$\frac{1}{2}$cm (4–5in) in diameter; the edges must be uniform in thickness.

5. Heat an ungreased pan over low heat, add one pair of pancakes at a time and cook each side until light brown. Remove from the pan.

6. Tear each pair apart to separate them and pile the pancakes on top of each other; cover with a damp cloth. Steam before serving.

Fillings:

Stir-fried Shrimp

450g (1lb) shrimps
1 teaspoon Chinese wine or dry
  sherry

1 teaspoon cornflour
3 teaspoons oil
½ teaspoon salt

1. Shell the shrimps and remove the veins, sprinkle with wine and cornflour.
2. Heat the oil; stir-fry the shrimps over a strong heat until the colour changes, add salt and serve hot.

Barbecued Pork Strips
Follow page 26

Scrambled Egg

Preparation time : 5 minutes   Cooking time : 5 minutes

3 eggs
¼ teaspoon salt

3 tablespoons oil

1. Beat the eggs and add the salt.
2. Heat the oil; when hot, pour in the egg mixture and cook, stirring constantly. Serve hot.

Stir-fried Bean Sprout

Preparation time : 5 minutes   Cooking time : 5 minutes

225g (8oz) bean sprouts
1 tablespoon Chinese wine or
  dry sherry

3 tablespoons oil
1 teaspoon vinegar
½ teaspoon salt

1. Wash the fresh bean sprouts or drain the canned bean sprouts.

2. Heat the oil, stir-fry the bean sprouts, add the wine, vinegar and salt, mix and serve.

Deep-fried Shredded Potato

Preparation and cooking time : 10 minutes

2 medium-sized potatoes   salt
oil for deep-frying

1. Peel the potatoes, slice and shred; wash, rinse and wipe dry with a paper towel.
2. Heat the oil and deep-fry a quarter of the shredded potato at a time. Stir to prevent from sticking together. When the colour changes to golden brown remove and sprinkle with salt.

Shredded Leek

7½cm (3in) leek per person
   shredded finely and served raw

Stir-fried Vermicelli

Preparation time : 20 minutes   Cooking time : 5 minutes

110g (4oz) dried vermicelli   3 tablespoons oil
2 teaspoons soy sauce or ¼   ½ cup water
   teaspoon salt

1. Soak the vermicelli in lukewarm water for 20 minutes, drain.
2. Heat the oil and stir-fry the vermicelli; add the soy sauce or salt and the water, cook until the water has evaporated.

Soy Bean Paste

2 tablespoons oil	½ tablespoon soy sauce
2 tablespoons sugar	½ cup soy bean paste
1 teaspoon Chinese wine or dry sherry	7½cm (3in) leek per person

1. In a small bowl combine the sugar, soy sauce, wine and bean paste. Heat the oil in a pan; add the bean paste mixture and cook over a medium heat until air bubbles appear. Cool and serve. Canned Hoisin Sauce may be used instead of this soy bean paste.
2. Cut the leeks into twelve 7½cm (3in) pieces. Shred one end with a sharp knife. Drop the leeks into cold water and soak until the shredded ends open like a flower. This 'leek flower' is used for decoration and it is also used as a brush when brushing the soy bean paste onto the pancake.

TO EAT:

1. Place a pancake on a serving plate. Using the 'leek flower' spread some soy bean paste lightly over one third of the pancake. Place the 'leek flower' on the centre of the pancake. Add any of the other ingredients, as you wish.
2. Fold the pancake once across the centre. Holding this in place, fold over the two sides, then roll into a tube. Hold the pancake in your hand and eat.

These pancakes may be served with stir-fried pork, eggs or Roast Duck.

Fried Rice

CHAO FAN

Preparation and cooking time : 45 minutes

2 cups rice	a pinch of salt
225g (8oz) pork meat (pork chop or rib eye steak)	5 tablespoons oil
110g (4oz) onion	2 teaspoons Chinese wine or dry sherry
110g (4oz) green pepper	2 tablespoons soy sauce
2 eggs	a dash of black pepper

1. Cube the pork meat and also the onion and green pepper.
2. Heat 4 tablespoons oil; stir-fry the onion and pork. When the pork changes colour remove to a plate.
3. Wash the rice and rinse with water 4 or 5 times until the water is clear; put in a pot.
4. Add 2 cups of water to the rice or follow the directions on the packet.
5. Add the stir-fried onion and pork, the wine, soy sauce, and black pepper. Cook until the water disappears.
6. Add the green pepper and simmer for another 10 minutes.
7. Heat 1 tablespoon oil; scramble the eggs with a pinch of salt, and stir this into the rice and serve.

Fried Rice with Egg

TAN CHAO FAN

Preparation time : 10 minutes   Cooking time : 15 minutes

4 cups rice	a dash of pepper
2 eggs	½ cup cubed ham
¾ teaspoon salt	4 tablespoons oil

1. Wash the rice several times until the water runs clear.
2. Drain and add an equal amount of water and cook.
3. As soon as the water boils turn down the flame. Simmer

until all the water is absorbed; let stand for 10 minutes or more to cool.

4. Heat 2 tablespoons oil; scramble the eggs and remove to a platter.

5. Heat 2 tablespoons oil; stir-fry the rice slowly until the oil coats all the grains. Add the cubed ham and egg, stir and serve.

Note : Left-over cool rice is good for this dish.

Fried Rice with Assorted Meats

SHH JUN CHAO FAN

Preparation and cooking time : 45 minutes

3 cups of cooked rice	6 shrimps
2 eggs	2 teaspoons green peas
85g (3oz) bamboo shoots	5 tablespoons oil
2 slices of ham	salt
1 dried or fresh mushroom	a dash of pepper
½ cup chopped leek or onion	

1. Place the cool rice in a mixing bowl. Separate the large lumps with a wooden spoon.

2. Cut the bamboo shoots into ¾cm (¼in) cubes. Rinse the green peas with hot water and drain. Dice the ham to the same size.

3. Chop the leek finely.

4. Shell the shrimps, remove the veins, and boil for 3 minutes. Remove from the water and cool.

5. Soak the dried mushroom until softened. Cut off the stem and discard. Dice the same size as the bamboo shoots.

6. In a bowl beat the eggs very well with a dash of salt and pepper.

7. Heat 2 tablespoons of oil in a pan. Stir-fry the eggs quickly until set and no longer glossy. Break the egg up finely. Set aside.

8. Add 1 tablespoon oil to a pan and heat over medium flame.

Stir-fry the leeks for 1 minute until wilted and fragrant. Raise the flame to high, add the bamboo shoots, ham, mushroom, green peas in that order, stirring after each addition. This should take no more than $1\frac{1}{2}$ minutes. Place on a warm plate.

9. Heat the last 2 tablespoons oil in the pan. Gently stir-fry rice to break up the small lumps into separate grains. Shake the pan as you stir-fry in order to keep the rice from burning.

10. When the rice grains are very hot, add the other cooked ingredients and continue to cook and stir until all is very hot and well blended.

11. Add about $\frac{1}{2}$ teaspoon salt to taste, and toss again to blend, very quickly. Serve hot.

How to cook rice. To make 3 cups of cooked rice: $1\frac{1}{2}$ cups uncooked rice; $1\frac{1}{2}$ cups water. Wash the rice to remove excess starch. Rinse several times until water is clear. Place rice in a pan with a fitting lid. Add the $1\frac{1}{2}$ cups of cold water. Bring to the boil, reduce heat and cook uncovered over medium to low flame until all the liquid appears to be absorbed. Place the lid on the pan. Turn heat to *very* low and cook for 20 minutes. The last step is a steaming process and if the flame is high the rice will burn. When this step is finished the rice should be tender but firm to the taste. If the rice is too soft, it will not make good fried rice.

The Chinese eat rice at each meal in the same manner as other people eat bread. There are many different kinds of rice including long grain, oval grain, short grain, glutinous and so forth. Some types absorb more water than others. The proportion of rice to water can vary as much as 1 cup of rice to 1 cup of water and 1 cup of rice to 3 cups of water. Whatever type of rice you buy, cooked, it should be neither too hard nor too soft; it should be dry with the moisture absorbed into each grain.

Notes : If raw green peas are used, they should be parboiled in slightly salted water to lightly cook them and also to give them a bright green colour.

The ingredients cook more evenly if they have been diced the same size.

The pan should be washed between steps in the cooking.

Steamed Shau Mai

CHENG SHAO MAI

Cooking time : 40 minutes

25 sheets Shau Mai wrappers* (skins)	1 tablespoon soy sauce
225g (8oz) minced pork	¾ teaspoon salt
110g (4oz) crab meat (canned, frozen or fresh)	1 teaspoon sugar
	1 tablespoon sesame oil
½ onion	1 tablespoon cornflour
1 tablespoon Chinese wine or dry sherry	25 green peas
	a little oil to brush on bottom of steamer

1. Remove the gristle from the crab meat. Squeeze to remove excess moisture.
2. Chop the onion very finely.
3. Parboil the green peas in slightly salted water. Rinse in cold water.
4. In a mixing bowl combine the minced pork, crab meat, chopped onion, wine, soy sauce, salt, sugar, cornflour, sesame oil, and mix thoroughly for the filling.
5. Place a Shau Mai wrapper in the palm of your left hand and cup it loosely. Place 1 tablespoon of filling in the centre of the cupped wrapper.
6. Close the left hand slowly and with the help of the right hand press the wrapper snuggly around the filling. The top stays uncovered.
7. Place the Shau Mai in between the thumb and index finger, squeeze the middle gently to give the cylinder a faintly wasp-waisted look.
8. Press lightly both top and bottom with the right hand to flatten the shape.
9. When all the dumplings are made, place one green pea on the top of each one.
10. Grease the bottom of the bamboo steamer rack to prevent sticking. Place the Shau Mai about 1cm (½in) apart on the rack.
11. Place the bamboo steamer rack, with cover, over a Chinese

wok (pan) filled with water up to 2½cm (1in) below the rack. When steam rises and is visible, steam over medium heat for 14 minutes.

12. Serve steamed Shau Mai accompanied by mustard, soy sauce, vinegar, and mix as preferred.

Notes: *It is best to keep the Shau Mai wrappers under a dampened, well-squeezed cloth to keep them from drying out. They will not pleat if allowed to dry.*

Instead of greasing the bottom of the bamboo steamer rack, a piece of dampened cheese cloth may be placed in the bottom of the rack.

Step 11 uses the Chinese wok (pan) and the bamboo steamer. If a metal steamer is used, there are some precautions to take:

1. *Do not put too much water in the steamer. If the water boils up on to the Shau Mai they will be watery and will not hold together.*
2. *Bring the water in the steamer to a rapid boil.*
3. *Turn the flame down so that the water is very lightly boiling or simmering.*
4. *Place the rack in the steamer and put the Shau Mai on it.*
5. *Cover the lid of the steamer with a cloth that can be tied over the top of the cover. This is to absorb the moisture that would normally collect on the underside of the lid and drop back into the pan. Place the cloth covered lid on the steamer.*

* *If you are unable to buy these, see below for recipe.*

Shau Mai Wrappers

1 cup self-raising flour   *1 cup cornflour*

Roll 1 tablespoon of Shau Mai filling (see page 110) lightly in the cornflour, then spray with water. Now roll the filling in the flour and spray with water. Repeat three or four times to form a thin coating.

Soups

Abalone Soup

PAO YU TANG

Preparation time : 20 minutes   *Cooking time : 10 minutes*

(A)
2 pieces canned abalone
2 slices ham
12 pieces bamboo shoots
5 button mushrooms
12 snow peas
6 quail eggs (optional)

6 cups broth
2 teaspoons salt
1 tablespoon Chinese wine or dry sherry
a dash of pepper
1 tablespoon melted chicken fat or sesame oil

1. Cut the abalone and ham into 5cm (2in) squares.
2. Slice the mushrooms into 5 or 6 pieces each.
3. Remove the ends and strings from the snow peas.
4. Boil the quail eggs and shell.
5. Heat the broth. Add (*A*) ingredients and seasonings, and bring to the boil.
6. Before serving, add the chicken fat or sesame oil to the soup for flavouring.

Assorted Meats Soup

SZU PO TANG

Preparation time : 20 minutes   Cooking time : 10 minutes

110g (4oz) chicken meat
about 2 tablespoons Chinese wine
  or dry sherry
1 teaspoon cornflour
225g (8oz) shrimps

½ cup button mushrooms
6 snow peas
6 cups water or broth
1 tablespoon salt
pepper

1. Slice the chicken and sprinkle it with 1 teaspoon wine and ½ teaspoon cornflour.
2. Shell the shrimps and de-vein. Sprinkle with ½ teaspoon wine and ½ teaspoon cornflour.
3. Slice the button mushrooms crosswise.
4. Wash the snow peas and remove strings.
5. Heat the broth; add 1 tablespoon wine and all the ingredients. Bring to the boil. Serve hot.

Cauliflower Soup

TSAI HUA TANG

Preparation time : 20 minutes   *Cooking time : 10 minutes*

225g (8oz) cauliflower (about
    1 head)
2 dried or fresh mushrooms
1 leek
60g (2oz) chicken fillet
2 egg whites

2 tablespoons oil
4 cups broth
1½ teaspoons salt
a dash of black pepper
3 tablespoons cornflour
6 tablespoons water

1. Separate the flowerets of the cauliflower from the stem and parboil.
2. Soak the dried mushrooms for 15 minutes. Remove the stems and chop.
3. Cut the leek into small pieces.
4. Chop the chicken fillet very finely.
5. Beat the egg whites until stiff and mix with the chopped chicken fillet.
6. Heat the oil in a pan and stir-fry the cauliflower, mushrooms and leek; add the broth and bring to the boil.
7. Add the salt, black pepper, and cornflour and water mixture, stir and bring to the boil.
8. Blend the chicken mixture into the broth; bring to the boil then serve.

Chicken Broth and Bone Broth

CHI TANG KU TO TANG

Preparation and cooking time : about 1 hour

1 chicken, or the bones from one
    chicken
10cm (4in) leek

4 slices ginger
8 cups water

1. Wash the bones in running water and then soak in sufficient water to extract the blood. Drain.

2. Put the bones into a deep pot and add 8 cups of water. Add the ginger and leek, and bring to a boil without a cover on the pan.

3. Remove the scum which rises to the surface. Reduce the flame and simmer for 40 minutes. From time to time remove any more scum which rises.

4. Strain carefully into a large bowl. Discard bones, leeks and ginger. Chill.

5. Pour stock into containers and cover. Keep in the fridge for up to 24 hours, or if the stock is not to be used immediately it may be frozen.

Note : Chinese soups are varied from simple to complex. For a simple soup, according to taste, add cooked sliced meat or sea food, vegetables and seasonings.

Complex soups always require chicken broth. The most famous are bird's nest soup and shark's fin soup. Every meal's soup is magnificent if chicken broth is used. It is simple to prepare and economical too.

Chinese Cabbage Soup

PAI TSAI TANG

Preparation and cooking time : 35 minutes

340g (12oz) Chinese cabbage	*salt*
15cm (6in) leek	*85g (3oz) vermicelli*
110g (4oz) pork, sliced	*5 cups stock or water*
2 tablespoons Chinese wine or dry sherry	*2 slices ginger*
	2 tablespoons oil
1 teaspoon soy sauce	*a dash of pepper*
1 teaspoon cornflour	

1. Cut the leek into 1cm ($\frac{1}{2}$in) thick sections.

2. Cut the cabbage into 2$\frac{1}{2}$cm (1in) square pieces.

3. Cut the pork into 2$\frac{1}{2}$cm (1in) square pieces. Combine 1 tablespoon wine, soy sauce, the cornflour and a pinch of salt; marinate the pork for 2–3 minutes in this mixture.

4. Place the vermicelli in a bowl and cover with lukewarm water. Soak for about 15 minutes until soft. Drain. Cut into 12½cm (5in) lengths.

5. Heat the oil in a pan; stir-fry the leek, ginger and pork over a strong heat until the pork changes colour. Add the soup stock or water and bring to the boil over a high heat. Reduce heat and continue cooking for 10 minutes. Add the cabbage.

6. Add the vermicelli. Turn the heat up and quickly bring to a fast boil. Add 1 tablespoon wine, 1 teaspoon salt and a dash of pepper. Remove from the heat and serve immediately.

Note : The cabbage will cook uniformly if the core portion of the leaf is cut smaller than the leaf portion.

If Japanese vermicelli is used the water should be lukewarm otherwise the vermicelli will be too soft. Chinese vermicelli can be soaked in boiling water. Do not continue boiling after the vermicelli has been added. Switch off the flame immediately after seasonings are added. Cabbage, spinach or cucumber can be substituted for Chinese cabbage.

Congee

CHOU

Preparation and cooking time : 1 hour 20 minutes

1 cup rice	2 teaspoons ginger juice or grated
8 cups water	ginger
225g (8oz) chicken fillet	1 tablespoon Chinese wine or
2 mushrooms fresh, dried or	dry sherry
canned	1½ teaspoons salt
225g (8oz) green leafy	a dash of pepper
vegetable, such as spinach	1 tablespoon soy sauce (optional)

1. The rice must be prepared first. Wash the rice and allow it to sit in the strainer for 30 minutes.

2. Remove the thin skin of the chicken fillet and remove the muscle. Dice the chicken into 1cm (½in) cubes. If the fillets are too thick, cut them in half and then slice.

3. If using dried mushrooms soak them in lukewarm water. Remove and discard the stems. Cut the mushrooms into 1cm (½in) lengths.

4. Place the drained rice in a large pan, add 8 cups of water and bring it to the boil over a strong heat. Turn the flame down and slowly boil for 40 minutes.

5. Add the chicken fillets, mushrooms, greens, ginger juice, wine, salt, pepper and soy sauce to the rice. Continue to boil for 10 minutes or until the mixture has thickened.

6. Transfer to a casserole or soup tureen. Serve in small individual bowls.

Note : Any kind of meat may be substituted for the chicken, such as beef, pork, kidney, liver, shrimp or abalone. Other vegetables may be used to add variety to the congee. The congee may be cooked in a flameproof casserole.

Egg Flower Drops Soup with Lettuce

TAN HUA TANG

Preparation and cooking time : 15 minutes

225g (8oz) pork, sliced
2 teaspoons Chinese wine or
   dry sherry
2 teaspoons soy sauce
2 teaspoons cornflour
4 tablespoons oil

½ stalk leek, cut into small pieces
12 pieces of lettuce, about 3 or 4
   leaves
8 cups broth or water
2 eggs, lightly beaten
½ teaspoon salt

1. Dredge the pork slices with the wine, soy sauce, and cornflour.
2. Heat the oil in a deep pan and fry the pork with the leek.
3. When the pork turns brown, add the broth.
4. After the soup comes to the boil, add the lettuce and salt.
5. Slowly stir in the beaten egg.

Note : Chicken or beef may be substituted for pork.

Fire Kettle

HUO KOU TZU

Preparation and cooking time : 1 hour

(A)
225g (8oz) chicken
7½cm (3in) leek cut into sections
1 piece of ginger about $\frac{1}{16}$cm
    (⅛in) thick, sliced into slivers

(B)
170g (6oz) minced pork
1 teaspoon grated ginger
1 tablespoon finely chopped
    leek
1 egg lightly beaten
1 teaspoon Chinese wine or dry
    sherry
¼ teaspoon salt
1 teaspoon cornflour
oil for deep-frying

(C)
3 tablespoons dried shrimps
½ cup dried scallops
110g (4oz) ham
60g (2oz) vermicelli
20 snow peas
4–5 dried mushrooms
110g (4oz) bamboo shoots
5 cabbage leaves
3 tablespoons chopped leek
1 tablespoon chopped ginger
2 teaspoons salt
2 tablespoons Chinese wine or
    dry sherry
5–6 cups soup stock

1. Boil the (A) ingredients in 4 cups of water for about 30 minutes until the chicken is tender; remove the foam from the top as it cooks. Remove the chicken from the broth and cool. With a knife, carefully remove the meat from the bones in large pieces; cut into slices approximately 1cm (½in) by 15cm (6in). Strain and skim the grease from the broth; keep for the soup stock.
2. Combine the (B) ingredients (except the oil) well together. Form into 8 balls. Heat the oil for deep-frying to medium heat. Fry the pork balls until lightly browned. Drain.
3. Place the dried shrimps and scallops in a small bowl and pour 1 cup of lukewarm to cool water over them; soak until tender. Drain, saving liquid to use as stock. Slice the ham into pieces 2½cm (1in) by 7½cm (3in) in size.
4. Cut vermicelli with scissors into 12½cm (5in) lengths;

place in a medium-sized mixing bowl. Pour over about 3 cups of lukewarm to hot water. Soak for about 15 minutes until tender then drain off the water.

5. String and wash the snow peas. Bring 2 cups of water to a rapid boil with ½ teaspoon salt. Drop in the snow peas for 1 to 2 minutes – no more. Strain and pour over cold water to stop them cooking further. They should be a brilliant green. Do *not* overcook.

6. Soak the mushrooms for about 15 to 20 minutes in enough lukewarm water to cover them. Drain off the water and keep it. Cut off and discard the stems. Slice the mushroom caps into ½cm (¼in) pieces.

8. Wash the cabbage leaves and shake off excess moisture; slice into 2½cm (1in) wide and 15cm (6in) long pieces.

To arrange food in the fire kettle :

9. In the bottom of the fire kettle place the 3 tablespoons chopped leek and 1 tablespoon chopped ginger.

10. Next, distribute the softened dried shrimps and scallops in the kettle. Place the cabbage leaves over all and the vermicelli on top of the cabbage.

11. On top, arrange the sliced ham, sliced mushrooms, meat balls, sliced bamboo shoots, snow peas and sliced chicken, each in its own section.

12. Make 5–6 cups of soup stock with the broth from the chicken, shrimps and scallops, and mushrooms. Add 2 teaspoons salt and 2 tablespoons wine and mix. Pour part of this soup stock over the ingredients in the fire kettle; the amount will vary according to the size of the pan. Add more stock as necessary.

13. Place some charcoal in the chimney of the fire kettle; keep the pot bubbling at all times. Red charcoal sparks should appear. Cook until all the food is very, very hot. Guests remove pieces of food from the fire kettle as they wish and dip them into condiments of their choice. An egg may be broken into the broth and poached for each person at the end if desired. The remaining broth can be placed into small bowls or cups for drinking at the end of the meal.

The firepot (fire kettle) is usually made of shiny brass with a chimney in the centre surrounded by a container to hold the ingredients and the stock. An electric deep-fryer or wok may be substituted.

There are many ways to serve from a fire kettle. The Chinese name *Ho go*, stove party, is a whole meal in which all of the food preparation has been done in advance. The soup stock is brought to a boil in the fire kettle. Guests pick up one piece of food at a time, from plates on the table, and cook them in the hot soup. Each guest then dips each piece into the condiments which he has mixed in his own bowl and eats it, then cooks another and so on.

One style is called Chrysanthemum Pot because of the white chrysanthemum petals which are used. So different foods are prepared and this style is only served as a last course as soup.

After the meal, pour a bowl of water into the chimney to put out the fire.

Note : There are two kinds of vermicelli. Read the instructions on the label, as one kind will become much too soft in hot water and lukewarm water must be used, the other needs lukewarm to hot water.

Fish Slice Soup

YU PIEN TANG

Preparation and cooking time : 25 minutes

225g (8oz) white fish	about 1 tablespoon Chinese wine
1 egg	or dry sherry
1½ teaspoons cornflour	½ teaspoon salt
1½ teaspoons flour	½ teaspoon ginger juice
1 cup sliced cucumber	a dash of pepper
6 mushrooms	oil for deep-frying
2½ cups stock or water	

1. Remove the skin from the fish. Slice the fish into bite-sized pieces.

2. Beat the egg lightly in a bowl, add 1 tablespoon wine, the cornflour, and the flour. Combine well. Place the fish in the mixture and coat thoroughly.

3. Heat oil for deep-frying over a medium heat to 160C/320F. Drop the batter-coated fish pieces in the oil one by one, and fry until light golden brown. Drain well.

4. Wash the cucumber, and cut it diagonally into very thin pieces.

5. Cut the mushrooms in half, or slice into thin pieces.

6. Boil 2½ cups of stock or water in a pot, bring to the boil and add the fried fish.

7. Add the cucumber slices, mushroom slices, ½ teaspoon wine, salt, dash of pepper and ginger juice. Bring to the boil. Serve the soup in a preheated container.

Note : If the temperature of the oil is too high, the fish tends to burn, and the soup will not look clear. If too many pieces of fish are fried at one time, the temperature of the oil drops, causing the fish to taste oily.

Fish Soup

YU TANG

Preparation time : 15 minutes   Cooking time : 15 minutes

225g (8oz) fish fillet
1 tablespoon Chinese wine or
  dry sherry
1 teaspoon salt
1 tablespoon cornflour
¼ cup carrot

¼ cup bamboo shoots
2 dried mushrooms or ¼ cup fresh
  mushrooms
6–8 cups broth
a dash of pepper

1. Cut the fish fillet into bite-sized pieces and sprinkle with wine, ½ teaspoon salt and cornflour.

2. Soak the dried mushrooms in lukewarm water; remove the stems and cut these, or the fresh mushrooms, into 4.

3. Slice the carrot and bamboo shoots.

4. Heat the broth; when boiling add the carrot, bamboo

shoots, ½ teaspoon salt, and mushrooms; bring to the boil and when the carrot is tender, add the fish and bring to the boil again. Serve.

Liver Soup

KAN KAO TANG

Preparation time : 30 minutes   Cooking time : 10 minutes

225g (8oz) chicken liver
1 tablespoon Chinese wine or
*   dry sherry*
a dash of black pepper
2 egg whites

170g (6oz) chicken fillet or
*   breast*
5½ cups chicken broth
1½ teaspoons salt

1. Wash the liver and chop finely; add 1½ cups cold broth and strain both through a sieve into a bowl.
2. Beat the egg whites until stiff and blend in the chopped liver. Remove to serving bowl and steam for 10 minutes.
3. To make the soup richer, chop the chicken fillet, add it to the 4 cups chicken broth and bring to the boil. Add salt and pepper; drain.
4. Before serving pour the rich soup into the steamed liver, and steam for 10 minutes. Serve hot.

Pork and Spinach Soup

PO TSAI JOU PIEN TANG

Preparation time : 20 minutes   Cooking time : 10 minutes

110g (4oz) sliced pork
1 teaspoon Chinese wine or dry
*   sherry*
1 teaspoon soy sauce
½ teaspoon cornflour
5 tablespoons oil
1 egg

60g (2oz) transparent
*   vermicelli*
110g (4oz) spinach
5 cups water
2¼ teaspoons salt
a dash of pepper
a dash of sesame oil

1. Shred the pork; mix with the wine, soy sauce and cornflour.
2. Heat 2 tablespoons oil in a pan. Fry the meat, and when it changes colour, remove to a plate.
3. Beat the egg and add ¼ teaspoon salt.
4. Heat 3 tablespoons oil. Make a thin egg sheet. Shred it.
5. Soak the transparent vermicelli for ten minutes in warm water, or overnight in cold water. Cut into 7½cm (3in) lengths.
6. Cook the spinach in boiling water. Rinse and drain. Cut into 5cm (3in) lengths.
7. Boil 5 cups water and add the pork. Bring to the boil.
8. To the boiling soup, add the spinach and shredded egg and bring to the boil again. Add the seasonings and sesame oil. Serve hot.

Shark's Fin Soup

YU CHI TANG

Should be prepared the night before   Cooking time : 1 hour

225g (8oz) dried shark's fin
170g (6oz) chicken meat
¼ cup ham
3 leeks
2 slices ginger
6 cups broth
2 tablespoons Chinese wine or
   dry sherry

1 tablespoon vinegar (optional)
½ teaspoon salt
a dash of pepper
2 tablespoons cornflour
2 tablespoons water

1. Use dried and refined cake-shape shark's fin; boil with leek and ginger for 30 minutes. Soak overnight.
2. Drain, wash, and rinse several times.
3. Shred the chicken meat into strips.
4. Bring the broth to the boil; add the shark's fin and simmer for 30 minutes. Add the chicken and simmer for an additional 20 minutes. Add the ham and seasonings.
5. Thicken the soup with a mixture of cornflour and water. Serve hot.

Shredded Chicken Soup

CHI SSU TANG

Preparation time : 20 minutes   Cooking time : 10 minutes

170g (6oz) shredded chicken
1 teaspoon Chinese wine or dry
sherry
1 teaspoon cornflour
2 eggs

1 teaspoon oil
6 cups chicken broth
a pinch of salt
a dash of black pepper

1. Marinate the shredded chicken with wine and cornflour.
2. Beat the eggs and add a pinch of salt. Heat a frying-pan, rub with a little amount of oil and make 2 thin pancake-like sheets of egg. Cut into the same lengths as the chicken and shred.
3. Heat the broth and add the chicken. When boiling, add the shredded egg. Serve.

Special Bean Curd Ball Soup

TOU FU WON TANG

Preparation time : 30 minutes   Cooking time : 10 minutes

1 cake bean curd
3 tablespoons shredded carrot
2 tablespoons shredded
mushroom
1 tablespoon sesame seeds
2 tablespoons vermicelli
1 egg white

1½ tablespoons cornflour
oil for deep-frying
6 cups broth
1 teaspoon sugar
1 teaspoon soy sauce
salt

1. Boil the shredded carrot, mushroom, and vermicelli until tender; drain.
2. Break the bean curd up with a whisk and add all the ingredients, except for the oil and broth.

3. Form teaspoon- or tablespoon-sized balls with the mixture.
4. Heat the oil and deep-fry the balls until golden brown.
5. Heat the broth and add the bean curd balls; serve.

Note : Fried bean curd balls will keep in the refrigerator for a week.

Thick Corn Soup

SU MI TANG

Preparation and cooking time : 10 minutes

1 cup of canned corn	2½ cups water
¼ cup of chopped ham	1 tablespoon cornflour
1 egg	2 tablespoons cold water
½ teaspoon salt	

1. Chop the ham very finely. Set aside.
2. Beat the egg well in a small bowl. Set aside.
3. Bring 2½ cups of water to a rapid boil; add the canned corn and bring to the boil again. Add ½ teaspoon salt.
4. Mix the cornflour with the cold water until dissolved, and add to the corn and water mixture while stirring constantly.
5. Slowly add the well beaten egg to the corn in a thin stream and mix lightly; turn off the flame. Turn out the soup into a preheated bowl. Sprinkle finely chopped ham over the top.

Note : The egg will not spread if it is not well beaten. If a richer soup is preferred, you may use chicken stock instead of water.

Winter Melon Soup with Chicken Chunks

TUNG KUA CHI KUAI TANG

Preparation and cooking time : 40 minutes

340g (12oz) winter melon
340g (12oz) chicken, cut into
    4cm (1½in) pieces, bones
    included
8 cups water
½ onion, cut into small sections

3 dried or fresh mushrooms
3 slices ham, cut in 1cm (½in)
    widths
1 tablespoon Chinese wine or
    dry sherry
2½ teaspoons salt

1. Boil the chicken with the onion in 8 cups of water for 20 minutes.
2. Cut round the melon with a cutter, or cut into bite-sized pieces (about 24 pieces).
3. If using dried mushrooms, soak them in lukewarm water for 20 minutes; cut into pieces the same size as the melon.
4. Add the melon, mushrooms, ham and seasonings to the soup. Simmer for 15 minutes. Serve.

Desserts

Almond Jelly

HSIN JEN TOU FU

Preparation time : 30 minutes   *Cooking time : 40 minutes*

½ *agar agar* (7½g/¼oz), see note   *canned fruits : one kind or mixed,*
2½ *cups water*   *e.g. grapes, orange segments,*
4 *tablespoons condensed milk*   *cherries*
1½ *teaspoons almond essence*

1. Wash the agar agar in cold water to clean it. Soften it for 30
minutes in a little cold water. Drain the agar agar and squeeze

it to remove as much moisture as possible. Break into small pieces.

2. Bring $2\frac{1}{2}$ cups water to a rapid boil, stir in the agar agar pieces, then bring to a low boil, stirring constantly to dissolve the agar agar. Remove from the heat. (Be careful while agar agar is dissolving, as it will boil up very easily and if the pan is not large enough it will boil over.)

3. Drain the liquid through a *very* fine sieve or cheese cloth (do *not* press down on pieces which do not go through in straining) into a deep bowl. Add the condensed milk and almond extract; mix well. Place in the refrigerator for about 30 minutes until set. The jelly will begin to set while it is still very warm – *never* stir while it is setting.

4. When it is set, cut through the jelly with a knife to make diamond shapes. Remove to serving bowl and pour chilled fruit with all of the juice from the can over the top; simple sugar syrup may be added as well. Serve cold.

Note: Evaporated or fresh milk may be substituted for condensed milk; add sugar to taste.

Gelatine may be used instead of agar agar. Add slightly less liquid than the packet directions suggest so that the jelly will be firm enough to cut into diamond shapes.

Banana Dessert

HSIANG CHIAO

Preparation time : 25 minutes   Cooking time : 10 minutes

2 bananas	2 tablespoons flour
1 egg white	oil for deep-frying
2 tablespoons cornflour	2 tablespoons icing sugar

1. Peel the bananas and cut into four crosswise and slice each piece into two lengthwise.

2. Beat the egg white until stiff, add the cornflour and flour gradually.

3. Heat the oil to 150C/300F.

4. Mix the banana into the batter, pick out the pieces and add to the heated oil; deep-fry until the colour changes to light brown. Put on absorbent paper and then transfer to a serving plate. Sprinkle with icing sugar.

Deep-fried Apple with Honey

FUNG MI PIEN KUO

Preparation time : 20 minutes   Cooking time : 20 minutes

2 apples*   oil for deep-frying
1 egg   ½ cup honey
¾ cup flour   2 tablespoons sesame seeds
½ cup water or less   1 bowl iced water with a few
5 tablespoons oil   ice-cubes

1. Peel and core the apples; cut each into 12 pieces.

2. Beat the egg, add the water and gradually combine the flour and 1 tablespoon oil to make a smooth batter. Dip the apple pieces in to coat with the batter.

3. Heat the oil and deep-fry the coated apples until golden yellow; place on a platter. Generously oil the platter to keep the fruit from sticking and use as a serving plate.

4. Heat 4 tablespoons oil, add the honey and stir over a low heat until the mixture becomes syrupy. Add the fried apples and mix. Serve accompanied by a bowl of iced water. To eat pick up the apple with chopsticks or a fork and dip into the iced water to crystallize the syrup.

* Bananas may be used instead of apples ; use 3 small bananas.

Fried Sesame Cookies

CHA MA HUA

Preparation and cooking time : 45 minutes

2 cups flour

1 teaspoon black or white sesame
  seeds

2 tablespoons lard or cooking fat

1 egg

½ cup sugar

flour for the chopping board

oil for deep-frying

1. Beat the egg lightly.
2. Sift the flour into a mixing bowl. Add the sugar, sesame seeds, lard, and beaten egg. Mix well with a wooden spoon, adding a small amount of water if necessary, to make a pliable dough.
3. On a lightly floured board, knead the dough until it is smooth and elastic. The Chinese say that you should knead until the dough is as soft as an ear lobe.
4. Place the dough in a bowl and cover with a damp cloth. Let stand for 30 minutes.
5. On a lightly floured board, roll the dough into a rectangle or square ¼cm (⅛in) thick.
6. Cut the dough into rectangles 2cm (1in) wide and 5cm (2in) long.
7. Cut a line with a sharp knife through the centre of each rectangle about 1cm (½in) from each end. Do not cut all the way to the ends. Fold one end toward the centre, pass it through the cut in the centre and carefully pull it right through. The strips in the centre will have a twisted ribbon effect.
8. Deep-fry until golden brown. Drain. Sesame cookies keep well in an airtight container.

Peking Delight Cake

PEKING TAN KAO

Preparation and cooking time : 1 hour 20 minutes

½ cup plain flour
1 cup strong plain flour
½ teaspoon baking powder
2 eggs
water
oil for deep-frying

1 cup sugar
3 tablespoons honey or molasses
1 teaspoon vinegar
1 tablespoon sesame seeds
2 tablespoons raisins
4 tablespoons peanuts

1. Sift the flour with the baking powder twice.
2. Mix with the eggs and 1 tablespoon or more of water and knead into a smooth dough; let stand for 30 minutes.
3. Roll the dough out to a thin sheet. Cut into strips like noodles, 5–7½cm (2–3in) long.
4. Heat the oil and deep-fry the noodles until golden brown and expanded. Remove and drain.
5. Grease the cake tin.
6. Cook the sugar with ¾ cup water, honey and vinegar over a medium heat until the 'hard-ball' stage – test by dropping a small amount of melted syrup into a cup of cold water and it should form a hard ball.
7. Add the deep-fried noodles to the syrup and mix until all the noodles are coated with syrup.
8. Pour the mixture into the mould; press hard until the cake is about 5cm (2in) high. Sprinkle the sesame seeds, raisins and peanuts over the top and let cool.
9. Cut into about eight squares and serve.

Steamed Chinese Cake

CHENG TAN KAO

Preparation and cooking time : 40 minutes

1 cup plain flour
1 teaspoon baking powder
4 eggs
100g (about 4oz) sugar

salad oil
candied fruit or dried coconut for
    decoration

1. Sift the flour and baking powder together.
2. In a medium-sized mixing-bowl beat the eggs until very thick and creamy. Gradually add the sugar and continue beating until the eggs and sugar double in volume.
3. Blend the flour into the egg mixture, a small amount at a time, turning the eggs over gently with a wooden spoon or spatula to maintain fluffiness.
4. Line the cake mould with greaseproof paper, or brush the mould with salad oil so that the cake can be easily removed.
5. Sprinkle some candied dried fruit, which has been shredded, or coconut, uniformly on the bottom of the mould. Slowly pour the batter into the mould. Remove the air bubbles that rise to the surface of the batter with a wooden spoon.
6. Steam over a medium-strong heat for 20 minutes.
7. Test to see whether the cake is cooked by inserting a cocktail stick or skewer into the centre of the cake. If no batter adheres, the cake is done.
8. Remove the cake carefully from the mould by turning it upside down on to a serving plate and cut into any desired shape. In Chinese style, the cake is usually cut into diamond shapes.

Note : It is wise to break each egg into a small bowl to check for spoilage before adding it to the mixing-bowl.

Fried Sweet Potato Balls Coated with Sesame Seeds

ZU MA PAI SHU

Preparation time : 10 minutes   Cooking time : 7 minutes

450g (1lb) sweet potatoes
8 tablespoons sugar
1 egg
2 tablespoons flour

6 tablespoons water
1 cup white sesame seeds
oil for deep-frying

1. Steam the sweet potatoes until very soft. Mash or strain through a sieve.
2. When cool, mix with sugar and egg.
3. Form small balls using a tablespoon.
4. Mix the flour and water; coat the sweet potato balls with the mixture and roll them in sesame seeds.
5. Fry the sweet potato balls in deep oil.

Note : This is an excellent dish to serve as a vegetable with turkey at Christmas.

Sweet Potatoes and Cherries

PAI SHU YING TAO

Preparation and cooking time : 25 minutes

¾kg (about 1½lb) sweet potatoes
1 can sweetened cherries
* (425g/15oz)*
1 teaspoon cornflour mixed with
* 1 tablespoon water*

(A)
1½ teaspoons lard or vegetable oil
2 tablespoons sugar
1 tablespoon honey
5–6 cups water

1. Peel the sweet potatoes and cut them into 5cm (2in) cubes.
2. Add the (A) ingredients to the sweet potatoes and boil for 20 minutes or until tender. Add the drained cherries and boil for another 5 minutes.

3. Arrange the sweet potatoes and cherries in a serving dish; thicken the juice with the cornflour mixture and pour over.

Note : If cooked in advance, steam to reheat before serving.

Suggested Menus

*Note : Any of the rice dishes in this book
are suitable for these menus.*

Menu for 2
Stir-fried Sliced Beef (*p. 20*)
Crab Fu Yung (*p. 77*)
Cauliflower Soup (*p. 114*)

Menu for 2
Sweet Meatballs (*p. 32*)
Stuffed Green Pepper with Fish Fillet (*p. 95*)

Menu for 4
Broiled Spare Ribs (*p. 29*)
Steamed Whole Fish (*p. 67*)
Fried Egg with Chopped Leek (*p. 79*)
Garlic Cucumber (*p. 94*)
Chinese Cabbage Soup (*p. 115*)

Menu for 4
Fried Chicken with Cashew Nuts (*p. 44*)
Prawn with Chilli Pepper (*p. 73*)
Braised Broccoli (*p. 88*)
Shredded Chicken Soup (*p. 124*)

Menu for 4
Smoked Fish (*p. 66*)
Steamed Cabbage Rolls (*p. 91*)
Thick Corn Soup (*p. 125*)

Menu for 4
    Fried Meat Pie (*p. 29*)
    Sweet and Sour Cucumbers (*p. 95*)
    Stir-fried Shrimp with Broccoli (*p. 75*)
    Egg Flower Drops Soup with Lettuce (*p. 117*)

Menu for 6
    Deep-fried Beef with Chilli (*p. 17*)
    Steamed Fish Roll (*p. 70*)
    Stewed Chicken with Taro Root (*p. 41*)
    Sauté Chinese Cabbage (*p. 90*)
    Pork and Spinach Soup (*p. 122*)

Menu for 6
    Chilled Noodle (*p. 100*)
    Fried Meatballs (*p. 31*)
    Sauté Oysters (*p. 72*)
    Abalone Soup (*p. 112*)

Menu for 6
    Fried Beef with Green Peppers (*p. 18*)
    Broiled Pork Loin (*p. 28*)
    Assorted Meats Soup (*p. 113*)
    Steamed Shau Mai (*p. 110*)
    Almond Jelly (*p. 127*)

Index

Kate Hendry

MEXICAN COOKERY TODAY

Kate Hendry lived in Mexico for two years while she collected the recipes for this book and talked with Mexican people about their cookery methods and eating customs.

The Mexican cuisine is exciting and vibrant. Hot fiery sauces, spilling with chiles and tomatoes, enliven fish, eggs and meat. Chocolate is a surprising yet perfect addition to poultry dishes. The delicious Guacamole is included with other avocado recipes; and tortillas are stuffed with beans and meat spiced with chile.

Kate Hendry has carefully adapted these recipes for the English kitchen while retaining their unique and authentic Mexican flavour.

Anne Theoharous

COOKING THE GREEK WAY

COOKING THE GREEK WAY offers the best of Greek cooking. Anne Theoharous has chosen the most delicious and most popular Greek recipes, such as Moussaka, Stuffed Vine Leaves and Baklava. She also includes some unusual traditional foods, and takes an entertaining look at Greek eating customs.

Anne Theoharous is of Greek origin and knows exactly how to prepare authentic Greek meals. Her well-tried and traditional recipes are presented in easy-to-follow steps and the more time-consuming dishes can be prepared in advance.

This is a book for everyone who wants to bring the true flavour of Greece into their home by cooking the Greek way.

Irma Goodrich Mazza

COOKING WITH HERBS

In **COOKING WITH HERBS** Irma Goodrich Mazza takes an adventurous and enthusiastic look at the use of herbs in cookery. If you've ever been tempted to add a sprinkling of herbs to a simple roast and been uncertain what to use, Mrs Mazza will give you lots of ideas. She provides complete information on growing and using twenty-five essential herbs. And her extensive range of imaginative and often simple recipes show how the use of herbs is a delicious but inexpensive way to add zest and variety to everyday ingredients.

COOKING WITH HERBS is for everyone who wants to use herbs more imaginatively.

Jean Conil

THE MAGNUM COOKBOOK

The Magnum Cookbook is a must for all serious cooks. It contains a wide variety of recipes ranging from the basic to exotic, as well as exciting recipes for special occasions. Roast beef and Yorkshire pudding and a host of other traditional English recipes are included.

Master Chef Jean Conil's experience as a chef and nutritionist has enabled him to write a comprehensive book covering all aspects of cookery. He outlines the basic 'do's' and 'don'ts' of which every cook should be aware; a knowledge which he hopes will give confidence and inspiration to develop new ideas in the kitchen.

Jean Conil has had a varied career as chef, restaurateur, author and teacher. He broadcasts regularly on LBC and has recently been appearing on BBC TV's 'Nationwide' programme.

Jan Hopcraft

COOKING TODAY, EATING TOMORROW

Do you like to cook for your friends but always find yourself too rushed to enjoy it? This bestselling cookery book is designed for busy people. The recipes are clearly presented in the form of menus for dinner, lunch and fork supper parties. No menu contains more than one dish which has to be made from start to finish on the actual day. Each recipe has been specially designed to cut right down on time spent in the kitchen at the last minute, so that you can enjoy more time with your guests.

ENTERTAINING ON A BUDGET

A practical guide to tempting yet inexpensive meals for entertaining. Jan Hopcraft demonstrates that lashings of wine and cream are not essential for a first-class meal. She uses cider and a wide range of herbs and spices to transform simple ingredients into delicious and exciting dishes. These imaginative recipes include totally new ideas as well as traditional dishes and advice on cutting costs. Many dishes can be prepared in advance, making this an essential cookery book for those who have to economise on time as well as cost.